Create a Gender-balanced Workplace

'Practical, ...ing, this book offers compelling
solutions to improve gender balance'
Hilary Spencer, Director, Government Equalities Office

'Workplace balance is a goal for all managers. None more important
than gender balance and this book describes why'
Sir Winfred Bischoff, Founding Chair, 30% Club; Chair,
Financial Reporting Council; Chair, J. P. Morgan Securities, plc

'Insightful and timely – Ann Francke's guide on why gender balance
matters at work is a must-read for all business leaders'
Brenda Trenowden, Global Chair, 30% Club

'Practical and informed guidance on the diversity imperative
and the diversity dividend'
Dame Cilla Snowball, former group Chairman and group CEO,
AMV BBDO; Chair, Women's Business Council, UK

'What a fantastic guide for getting ahead in business. Packed to
the brim with practical tips, this book clearly demonstrates how we
can work together to fix one of the biggest challenges we face at work.
An absolute must-read for any leader'
Vanessa Vallely, OBE, Managing Director, WeAreTheCity

'This is one of the most important issues we face and all of us
should ask how we can help make progress. This book offers
simple advice on what you can do to make a difference'
Paul Polman, former CEO, Unilever;
Impact Champion, HeforShe

'Ann ably demonstrates that while there is no silver bullet, there
are practices that help organizations achieve gender balance'
Vivian Hunt, Managing Partner, McKinsey &
Company, UK and Ireland

Ann Francke

Create a Gender-balanced Workplace

BUSINESS

PENGUIN BUSINESS

UK | USA | Canada | Ireland | Australia
India | New Zealand | South Africa

Penguin Business is part of the Penguin Random
House group of companies whose addresses can
be found at global.penguinrandomhouse.com.

First published 2019
004

Text design by Richard Marston
Set in 11.75/14.75 pt Minion Pro
Typeset by Jouve (UK), Milton Keynes
Printed and bound in Great Britain by
Clays Ltd, Elcograf S.p.A.

A CIP catalogue record for this book is available
from the British Library

ISBN: 978-0-241-39624-7

**Follow us on LinkedIn: linkedin.com/
company/penguinbusiness**

www.greenpenguin.co.uk

MIX
Paper from
responsible sources
FSC
www.fsc.org   FSC® C018179

Penguin Random House is committed to a
sustainable future for our business, our readers
and our planet. This book is made from Forest
Stewardship Council® certified paper.

For Izzy and Arden

Contents

List of figures

List of tables

Introduction

Why this book?

People often ask me why I am so passionate about gender equality at work. After all, as the CEO of the Chartered Management Institute, I could champion so many other management and leadership topics – from how to be agile and authentic to top tips for crafting purpose, strategy and trust. Some of my members challenge me about this when they see me tweet, give a talk or comment in the media about gender balance – all of which I do very frequently. So why care about this topic so much that I'm even writing a book about it? Despite a backlash that has seen CMI dismissed as 'just another fringe group . . . adopting feminist mantras of inequality and divisive strategies'. (The comments every time I blog for the *Daily Telegraph* on gender equality issues get far more abusive than this one.)

The answer is simple. CMI is all about helping people to be better managers and leaders at work – turning 'accidental managers' into 'conscious leaders'. And gender balance is one of the best levers we can pull to:

- develop better managers and leaders at every level
- improve line management skills
- enhance team performance, and
- create better cultures and business results.

First and foremost, gender balance is a business issue, and the case for it is compelling. To give you an idea of the 'size of the prize', McKinsey estimates that true gender balance at work could add $28trn to global GDP if we achieved it everywhere[1] – that's more than the GDPs of the USA and China combined.

But my interest isn't only commercial. It's also personal, a real passion of mine, born out of many instances in my career where I experienced it – or didn't. Each time, I can honestly say that true gender balance made a positive difference to results.

Sometimes we create balance by accident. When I was a category director at Procter & Gamble in the mid-nineties, I got a phone call out of the blue from the HR chief in the Cincinnati headquarters. She asked to come and visit my 'patch' of cosmetics and skincare in the UK. We had the highest market shares and profit margins anywhere for Olay globally, and she was keen to learn more. When we discussed what lay behind that success, we discovered that I had one of the most gender-balanced teams anywhere in P&G. I wish I could say it was intentional – it wasn't. But the environment we created as a result was. We had an authentic, challenging, trusting atmosphere where everyone could be their best selves, and we allowed everyone to work according to their own flexible schedule. Me, I was a divorced mum of one who needed to take her five-year-old daughter to school every day, while my direct reports had different considerations. One was a young male violinist in an orchestra who wanted to play first chair; there was a young woman on the netball team; and a twenty-something clubber who wanted to arrive late and leave late.

Fast-forward twenty years to my role as CEO of CMI, and I now have a gender-balanced executive team. And this time, it's by design. This book will help *you* build gender balance at work by design.

Many times I have experienced the downside of being the only woman on a senior team and the uncomfortable feeling of being 'other'. I've been:

- Excluded – 'Gentlemen, to the boardroom!' exclaimed the CEO to my male colleagues. I hesitated. Was I included or not?
- Belittled – 'Well, you're an American. A woman. Emotional. Very direct. Maybe you don't belong on the board of a British company.'
- Bullied – 'Who agrees with this woman?' bellowed the global CEO in a strategy meeting of the top twenty-five global leaders. I was the only female. Very few male hands went up.

I will explore many of the negative situations and behaviours that hold women back at work, and give advice on how to overcome them – whether you are on the receiving end, observing this behaviour from other colleagues, or maybe unwittingly doing it yourself. I will draw on the many examples I hear from women all over the world who have been affected.

But this book goes well beyond personal experiences and anecdotes. CMI has been at the forefront of exploring the gender pay gap for decades, and has championed gender balance ever since Eleanor Macdonald founded Women in Management (now CMI Women), back in 1969. We have been measuring the pay gap for many years, with XpertHR, and have advised the UK government on mandatory gender pay gap reporting – an innovative policy whereby companies with more than 250 employees have to publish their pay gaps on a government website every year.

I wish I could tell you there's been huge progress since

we started our measurements. But the reality is that the pay gap – and the percentage of women in senior management roles – has been pretty much stagnant over the past five years. The 'shape' of women in management continues to look like a pyramid: many more at the bottom, in junior roles, and fewer at the top in senior roles. We call this the 'glass pyramid', and it is the major cause of the gender pay gap, which is driven by the discrepancy in the number of women versus men in senior leadership roles. I will explore the current situation and the main causes of the gender pay and promotion gap in Chapter 2. We will also look at the differences by sector, and the role that bonuses and other perks play in widening the gap.

In the seven years I've been at CMI, the focus on gender pay equality has increased enormously. Before, mentions were few and far between. In recent years, there has been an explosion of campaigns, movements and coalitions to address this issue. There are countless high-profile examples, including the following.

- Me Too Movement (campaign against sexual harassment)
- 30% Club (campaigning for gender balance on boards)
- Davies Review (into increased representation of women on FTSE 100 boards)
- Hampton-Alexander Review (into the number of women in senior positions in FTSE 350 companies)
- WeAreTheCity (leading women's careers website, supporting female talent)
- Women Ahead (UK-wide business support community)
- Global Institute for Women's Leadership (tackling women's under-representation in leadership positions)
- HeForShe (solidarity campaign for the advancement of gender equality)

Awareness of gender as an issue has risen sharply among CEOs and leaders in general.[2] Over 80 per cent of FTSE 350 companies now have a gender diversity policy.[3] On any given day you'll find copious coverage in *The Times*, *Financial Times*, *Harvard Business Review*, *Forbes* and other business publications. The number of scholarly articles on this subject has doubled since 2010. And this doesn't include the vast array of practitioner studies from folks like McKinsey and PwC.[4] Many governments are now passing initiatives such as quotas for women on boards in Europe (something the state of California has now also adopted), and introducing the UK government's gender pay gap reporting requirement.

While much of this is welcome, it has also provoked what some call 'gender fatigue'. As one FTSE 100 chairman put it to me, 'I'm sick of talking about the gender gap. We've done that.'

But we haven't. Despite all the noise, there's really not been much constructive action. The World Economic Forum's 2018 report noted that the economic gap between women and men changed little in 2018 versus 2017 and will still take more than 200 years to close. Women are paid about 63 per cent of what men earn[5] and the number of women in leadership positions in large companies in 44 countries over the past two years has remained a paltry 5 per cent.[6]

There are pockets of progress but the truth is, conversations don't always inspire action to change culture or behaviours; indeed, they can reinforce bias and give rise to rhetoric, apathy or even backlash. These are some of the issues that get in the way of progress, and Chapter 3 is devoted to addressing them.

It's not all bad news. Now that so much attention is being directed at gender balance, practices are emerging that really work. If we can highlight these, and share the many success stories, we can build belief and momentum.

As is often the case with complex problems, there is no 'silver bullet'. But there are practices that deliver results. These occur at multiple levels, and very often involve collaboration between different types of organizations, such as business, government and campaigning organizations, as well as the media. I call this a 'coalition of the willing'.

Working together achieves much more than working in silos, and this is especially true when it comes to driving transparency and targets. In all cases, strong, authentic sponsorship from the organization's CEO and top leaders is essential. Targets are achieved by consistent implementation and measurement of practices and processes aimed at improving:

- recruitment
- retention and promotion rates
- sponsorship and mentoring, and
- flexible working policies.

Beyond targets, the real challenge is changing culture and behaviour – and this simply won't work unless men are included as champions of change alongside women. Finally, there is the role of government, society and education. Chapter 4 looks at all of these issues, and focuses on practical tips in each area so you can craft your own action plan, whether you are looking to do this at an organizational or team level.

In the end, we are all accountable when it comes to gender balance, and we can all contribute. So Chapter 5 focuses on what you as an individual – woman or man – can do to improve the gender balance where you work.

A few notes on the book's structure: I have gathered examples from many great sources with the aim of creating a practical, easy-to-use guide for you and your organization. I've organized things around the 'power of five' – five chapters, each with five key points. Alongside case studies and examples, you will find useful illustrations throughout that summarize the key findings of the book, which you can use to inform your own presentations or to share with others. At the end of each chapter (and peppered throughout) you'll find quotes from experts and champions in this field. And at the end of the book you'll find suggestions for further resources.

The objective of this book is to provide you with enough information and inspiration to take action. So all of the stories are real. In many of the most egregious examples, names of individuals and organizations have been changed. But that doesn't mean they didn't happen. They did, and it's important to include them. In my career, I've learned as much – if not more – from my bad bosses as from my good ones. This holds true for life in general: we learn more from our failures than we do from our successes.

Finally, I'd like to address an important issue up front. This short book is about gender balance. That doesn't mean that other forms of diversity like ethnicity, sexual orientation or disability aren't as important. They are – indeed, they're essential for creating better, more productive and inclusive societies and workplaces. But I've focused on gender because women are not a minority; they are more than 50 per cent of the world population. So it's a great place to start. There is also much more good data available on gender.

There's another compelling reason to concentrate on gender. Because the practices that address gender balance work for aspects of diversity, too.

In the end, it comes down to creating a culture where everyone feels trusted, able to be themselves and to contribute from their own unique perspective. For managers and leaders, it's about showing understanding and empathy, respect and a willingness to listen; about including and, yes, challenging and supporting.

So start with gender and I guarantee you'll make progress for the other groups as well. As the founder of the 30% Club, Dame Helena Morrissey, has often said, if you 'get' gender, you more readily 'get' other forms of diversity.

As I said at the outset, gender balance drives better managers and leaders, and better managers and leaders achieve better outcomes at an individual, team, firm and societal level.

So what are we waiting for?

Let's get started!

1 The Business Case for Gender Equality at Work

| Figure 1: 5 Benefits of Gender Balance

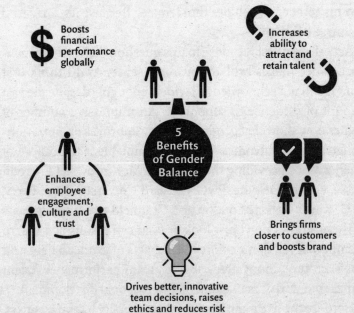

Boosts financial performance globally

Increases ability to attract and retain talent

5 Benefits of Gender Balance

Enhances employee engagement, culture and trust

Brings firms closer to customers and boosts brand

Drives better, innovative team decisions, raises ethics and reduces risk

> 'An inclusive and diverse business is not just a good thing
> to do. It is also a business imperative. A more diverse
> workplace is not just a better place to work. It makes us
> a better business, too.'
> – Ivan Menezes, CEO of Diageo[1]

I've been asked many times in interviews or on panels *why* we should try to close the gender pay gap. I often hear other people answer this question by saying that first and foremost it's the right thing to do, as part of an equal and fair society. Canadian Prime Minister Justin Trudeau famously replied, when asked why his cabinet was 50 per cent female, 'Because it's 2017.' And of course he's right.

Actually my first response to this question is always that gender balance makes brilliant business sense. And I think that point is still not acknowledged widely enough – despite the vast amount of evidence to support it. An impressive number of studies now show that gender diversity improves organizational metrics and outcomes. What's also notable is the calibre of organizations providing the evidence: McKinsey, MIT, Credit Suisse, Gallup, Deloitte, PwC, Harvard University, Korn Ferry, FRC, King's College London and Cranfield to name a few.

These studies don't just look at financial results at a macro and micro level; they explore the impacts of gender balance on ethics, culture, innovative capacity, team performance, talent management, risk management and personal development.

Here are the five main impacts that diversity has on business.

1 Boosts financial performance – globally and for firms
2 Enhances employee engagement and inclusive culture
3 Drives better, more innovative team decisions, raises ethics, reduces risk

4 Increases ability to attract and retain talent
5 Brings firms closer to customers and boosts brand

We're going to look at these in detail now. Where appropriate, I've included a simple infographic so you can summarize and share the evidence more easily. I've also added observations and examples where relevant.

1. Boosts financial performance – globally and for firms

Major studies demonstrate the value that equal economic participation of women in the workplace adds to the global economy. Two of the biggest are from the World Economic Forum

| Figure 2: The Financial Benefits of Gender Balance

$5.3trn Estimated increase in Global GDP by 2025 through closing the gender gap by 25%

 Professional services firms that switch from being all-male offices boost their revenues by 41%

 $28 trn added to global GDP if women participated equally in the economy to men

The Financial Benefits of Gender Balance

The most gender-diverse companies are 21% more likely to outperform their less diverse competitors

 Investors in more gender-diverse companies reaped an extra 3.5% CAGR in their returns

 Higher gender-diverse companies outperform their low-diversity peers and deliver higher return on equity

and McKinsey. Both highlight the enormous contribution to global growth that gender equality would yield.

The World Economic Forum (WEF) estimates that global GDP would increase by US$5.3trn by 2025 if we were to close the gender gap in economic participation by 25 per cent over that period.[2] The same report notes that the economic gender gap has improved only 2.5 per cent since 2006 and will take more than 200 years to close at the current rate. Interestingly, only 59 per cent of the economic gap between men and women is closed in the 149 countries covered by WEF's index, whereas in health and education the gap is closed at 95 per cent and 96 per cent respectively; the biggest gap is still in the political arena, where only 22 per cent is closed.[3]

McKinsey's figures for the potential GDP boost of closing the gender gap are equally bullish: the McKinsey Global Institute estimated in 2015 that $28trn would be added to global GDP by 2025 if women participated equally in the economy. That's an increase of 26 per cent – as big as the US and Chinese economies combined![4]

Okay, so there's not much you can do with those huge sums – except perhaps be sceptical about them – but it is noteworthy that so many elite organizations advising the world's CEOs (most of whom are not female) have come to this conclusion.

However, most readers won't be looking for evidence at a global level but rather something closer to home to improve the performance of their own organization.

Again, McKinsey offers some compelling numbers in the 2018 report 'Delivering through Diversity'. It turns out that companies in the top quartile for gender diversity on their executive teams are 21 per cent more likely to outperform their competitors in the bottom quartile. This finding is based on data from 1,000-plus companies in twelve countries. (Note that these results were for gender-diverse executive teams, not boards – albeit both are important.) The best performers also had more women in line management roles (with revenue and profit responsibility) than staff roles (HR, marketing, etc.).

The same study found an even higher performance boost – a whopping 35 per cent – for those with ethnically diverse teams.[5] An MIT study found that professional services firms that switched from being all-male or (more rarely) all-female offices boosted their revenues by 41 per cent.[6] As Dame Cilla Snowball, Chair of the Women's Business Council, told me, 'The bottom line is that diversity is good for everybody. Women and men.'

There appears also to be a financial 'diversity dividend'. The investment bank Morgan Stanley has concluded: 'Higher gender-diverse companies have outperformed their low-diversity sector peers for the past five years and deliver a slightly higher return on equity.'[7]

Credit Suisse looked at the performance of more than 3,000 companies globally. Again, it found that diversity paid dividends: investors in more gender-diverse companies reaped an extra 3.5 per cent compound annual growth rate in their returns versus their less diverse counterparts.[8] And MSCI, an investment services firm, examined US companies with at least three women on their boards and found that they had 10 per cent gains in return on equity and 37 per cent gains in earnings per share, while those with no female directors had declines in both measures over a five-year period. MSCI found the same basic pattern in a global snapshot of companies in 2015.[9]

The topic is moving beyond being just a 'women's issue', with increasing interest from investors. Many C-suite executives acknowledge that the main driver for diversity is the business case. Perhaps the most prescient and persistent leader in this space – an early proponent of 'the Future is Female' thinking – is another former P&G colleague of mine, Paul Polman, the ex-CEO of Unilever. He has achieved gender balance in Unilever's board and management team, as well as leading many external diversity initiatives for the UN and others, and believes that investing in equal opportunity for women and girls is number one of the UN's Sustainable Development Goals with the highest return for the global economy.[10] More and more global leaders agree. As Goldman Sachs CEO and Chairman David Solomon put it in an interview with Bloomberg, 'It's right, it's necessary, it's a business imperative, and it's my responsibility.'[11]

Let's look at the factors that underpin the financial results.

2. Enhances employee engagement and inclusive culture

Firstly, diverse environments create better engagement and trust. This, in turn, creates more inclusive cultures where people can be themselves and are able to perform better at work.

If diversity is about organizations representing a cross-section of groups, inclusivity is about enabling those individuals to feel welcome, listened to and able to contribute. Diverse companies tend to do a better job of creating these inclusive cultures.[12] And inclusive leaders are 84 per cent more likely to motivate their employees and improve their performance and productivity.[13]

When I reflect on my own executive career, I know that in every case where we've had gender, cultural and ethnic balance we've had a much more engaged environment, with everyone contributing more openly. And this is increasingly supported

| Figure 3: Engagement and Trust

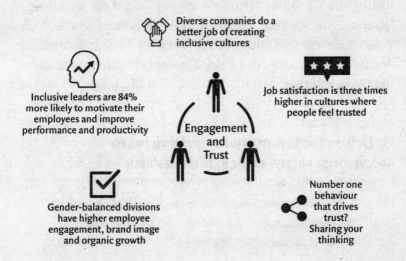

Diverse companies do a better job of creating inclusive cultures

Inclusive leaders are 84% more likely to motivate their employees and improve performance and productivity

Job satisfaction is three times higher in cultures where people feel trusted

Engagement and Trust

Gender-balanced divisions have higher employee engagement, brand image and organic growth

Number one behaviour that drives trust? Sharing your thinking

by research. CMI has found that job satisfaction is almost three times higher in cultures where people feel trusted – and firms where managers trust their leaders are much more likely to grow. What is the number one behaviour that drives trust? Sharing your thinking.[14] And having a diverse climate at work enhances trust.[15]

A study by the global service-provider Sodexo involving more than 50,000 employees found that gender-balanced divisions had higher employee engagement and brand image, as well as higher organic growth and profit.[16] After the firm increased the number of women from 17 per cent of the workforce in 2009 to 40 per cent (43 per cent of the board of directors are currently female), it saw a 4 per cent increase in employee engagement, a 23 per cent rise in gross profit, and brand image improved by 5 percentage points.[17]

I post often on LinkedIn about this topic and was delighted when a former P&G colleague of mine replied, remarking that five of his seven direct reports are women. He is Benno Dorer, the CEO of Clorox, a company famed for its positive and inclusive culture. Benno is also the best-rated CEO on Glassdoor. He told Bloomberg, 'There's a benefit to being a leader in this space, and I think companies are increasingly waking up to that.'

3. Drives better, more innovative team decisions, raises ethics, reduces risk

> 'A balanced management team leads to better decisions and the impact reverberates through the organization.'
> – Ivan Menezes, CEO of Diageo

There's a spate of evidence to show that diverse teams make better decisions, are smarter, more innovative and creative. Here's a quick snapshot.

- Teams with gender, age and geographic diversity make better business decisions 87 per cent of the time – whereas all-male teams only do this 58 per cent of the time.[18]
- A study of more than 1,800 professionals and 40 case studies in the USA demonstrated that teams with both inherent (i.e. gender, racial) diversity as well as acquired (i.e. experiential) diversity were 45 per cent more likely to outperform and out-innovate compared to those without these characteristics.[19]
- Similar findings were reached in a study of more than 4,000 firms in Spain, where the more diverse companies were also more innovative.[20]

| Figure 4: Innovation, Ethics and Risk

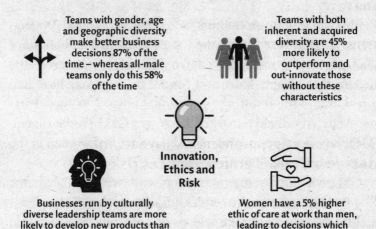

Teams with gender, age and geographic diversity make better business decisions 87% of the time – whereas all-male teams only do this 58% of the time

Teams with both inherent and acquired diversity are 45% more likely to outperform and out-innovate those without these characteristics

Innovation, Ethics and Risk

Businesses run by culturally diverse leadership teams are more likely to develop new products than those with homogenous leadership

Women have a 5% higher ethic of care at work than men, leading to decisions which are more rounded and less risky

What's going on here? Simply this: we work harder and smarter in diverse environments. We listen more, try harder to understand the facts, and process these thoroughly when making decisions. We increase our consideration of other points of view when the people sharing them come from a very different background to our own, and are more likely to allow others' perspectives to influence our opinions. This, in turn, makes us more likely to build on and create 'out of the box' breakthrough ideas and solutions.[21]

By contrast, when everyone comes from the same social and experiential background – say, white, middle-aged, male and Ivy League or Oxbridge – everyone is far more likely to think the same. And far less likely to challenge each other's decisions or introduce a different slant or perspective. As Sir Philip Hampton put it at the launch of the 2018 Hampton-Alexander Review, 'We are programmed to feel comfortable with our own tribe. People who look like us, dress like us, speak our language and so on . . .'

This can lead to 'groupthink' and boards making risky decisions. A report examining the top 20 corporate failures since 2000 (involving more than \$6trn of assets) discovered that the absence of 'soft skills' and gender balance may have had a real link to the resulting reputational crisis.[22] As PwC Partner Andy Woodfield remarked at a recent CMI Women event, 'Men have been overconfident and have not had women in the room who've said, "But are we sure . . . ?"'

CMI has done some interesting work with the academic Roger Steare, an expert in ethics, on why gender-diverse leadership groups might take less risky decisions. We find that women have a 5 per cent higher ethic of care at work than men, which means they have greater empathy and are more likely to consider the impacts on a broader group of stakeholders – customers, communities, employees – and take those into consideration.[23] That, in turn, can lead to decisions that are more rounded and less risky. (Maybe this more rounded attitude towards risk explains why a KPMG study found that hedge funds run by women delivered superior returns over time.[24]) When you consider recent corporate crises, such as at Tesco and Volkswagen, you see that an all-consuming drive for financial returns – coupled with unwavering commitment to a CEO's commercial imperative, and lack of challenge by senior managers – seems to lead to sub-optimal decision-making, ethical transgression and reputational crisis.

4. Increases ability to attract and retain talent

Whenever I hear senior leaders talk about the business case for greater diversity – which is often, if not daily – this is the first reason I hear them give: it's all about the ability to access the full talent pool. As Mark Read, CEO of WPP, told an audience of communications experts, 'Logically, if men and women are equally talented, we should be 50 per cent of the workforce all the way through . . . so obviously, yes, there is a business opportunity for WPP. If we can obtain a leadership position in this, we can attract better people, and that will make us more successful.'

| **Figure 5: Retaining Talent and Attracting Customers**

 Accessing the full talent pool is the top reason why leaders are interested in proving equality at work in both gender and ethnicity

 Women make up to 80% of purchase decisions so understanding how women might perceive a product or service is key

 An inclusive and collaborative culture is a retention driver for over 90% of women (above salary) – with flexible working and work–life balance the number one ask

 Retaining Talent and Attracting Customers

The number of CEOs focused on diversity in their talent pipeline has risen sharply to 87% (from 64% in 2015)

Diversity improves performance in call centres and retail outlets, leading to higher customer satisfaction scores

Access to skills is a top concern for leaders everywhere. PwC has found that 77 per cent of all CEOs cite lack of access to talent as the top threat facing their business.[25] The number of CEOs focused on diversity in their talent pipeline has risen sharply to 87 per cent – up from 64 per cent in 2015.[26] The challenges are particularly acute in areas such as STEM (science, technology, engineering and maths) and financial services, as we shall discover in Chapter 2.

Gender balance is increasingly becoming a key requirement for job candidates. Over 60 per cent of female hires expect companies to 'walk the talk' on their diversity practice and actively look at this when considering employment. Sadly, just under half – 46 per cent – think that women still face active gender bias in recruitment (something we will explore more closely in Chapter 3).[27]

When it comes to staying with an employer, having an inclusive and collaborative culture is a key retention driver for over 90 per cent of women (flexible working and work-life balance was the number one ask).[28] Both of these trumped salary as a reason to stay with an organization. Inclusive leadership, too, is a big loyalty booster for over 80 per cent of women.

Women are looking for role models as well – when they look up and don't see any women in the senior ranks, this throws up a real red flag.[29] And diverse employees are more likely to leave if they don't see people like themselves. Especially in rapidly growing economies, attracting and retaining women is a real challenge. Tailoring policies to appeal more towards women is a vital part of recruitment strategy. Those on the World's Most Admired Companies list, compiled by Fortune, have twice as many women in senior management as do those lower down.[30]

Ultimate Software, headquartered in Weston, Florida, is the number one large company on the list of great places to work

for women. It attracts technology talent all the way to South
Florida by offering benefits such as unlimited paid time off,
health and dental benefits and life insurance premiums fully
paid by the company, as well as a unique female leadership
programme that has yielded a 50/50 female-to-male employee ratio. 'The cost is minor compared to the outcome,' says
Ultimate's CFO. 'We have really low turnover and attrition is
somewhere around 5 to 6 per cent.'[31]

5. Brings firms closer to customers and boosts brand

In most product categories, women make around 70 to 80 per
cent of purchase decisions and are the fastest-growing audience of global consumers. By 2028 it's estimated that women
will control over 75 per cent of discretionary spending worldwide. As James Gorman, Chair and CEO of Morgan Stanley,
put it, 'Women live longer than men; more of the world's wealth
will ultimately be in the hands of women – that's real, that's
happening.'[32]

It makes compelling sense that we get moving to balance our
workforces so they reflect the composition of customer communities. A crucial part of building a better, more innovative
and customer-centric business is to understand how women
might approach your product or service. WPP's Mark Read
commented, 'We really started to pay attention [to gender di-
versity] when clients started to say to us, "Well, what are your
policies in this area? How are you promoting women in the
workplace?" '

For the Disney Company, attracting and retaining a diverse
workforce provides a deeper understanding of the needs of

the consumer, and has enabled the company to keep ahead of the market.[33] Diverse firms in professional and other service industries enjoy higher employee satisfaction, which leads in turn to higher customer and client satisfaction – some firms have even lost pitches by sending in all-male teams to clients. In call centres and retail outlets, it's been shown that diversity improves performance and leads to higher customer satisfaction scores.[34] Cressida Dick, the first female Police Commissioner for the London Metropolitan Police, aims to have 50 per cent of the force female (up from just under 30 per cent) because she wants her police force to reflect the community it serves.[35] Susan Story, CEO of American Water, agrees. She said, 'If you do not reflect your communities and the customers you serve, you are not optimizing your business performance. It is not only the right thing to do, but also the smart business strategy.'[36]

The diversity agenda is also affecting how brands are perceived. Recently Unilever revamped its Axe male-grooming brand to reflect a more sensitive, modern metrosexual. Famously, Dove's sales took off when the skincare brand started using real women in its marketing and campaigning for body positivity.

Brands are eliminating sexism in response to negative reaction. Clarks shoes changed their brand strategy after consumers complained that boys' shoes were black, sturdy and called 'Leader', whereas girls' shoes were pink, fluffy and called 'Princess'. Increasingly, consumers want to see modern society reflected in their brands, and they'll rapidly support products that meet this desire. Just look at *Good Night Stories for Rebel Girls*, a book that aims to revise perceptions of princesses for little girls and boys, and which became the fastest-funded entrepreneurial idea on Kickstarter in 2016 and has sold more than three million books worldwide.

In summary

Gender balance makes business sense. In this chapter we've looked at the business case for gender equality, and my hope is that by the end of it you have become convinced that it's a business no-brainer.

And there's a powerful societal imperative to work towards it too. Diversity delivers results against every organizational metric. On this basis you'd think we'd be hurtling full-steam towards a gender-balanced world of work.

But we are not.

In the next chapter we'll explore where we are now, and the main reasons for the lack of progress.

··

What Other Experts Say

How compelling is the business case for gender balance? How well do you think it is understood?

Dame Cilla Snowball (former group Chairman and group CEO, AMV BBDO; Chair, Women's Business Council, UK)

'I think, whilst everybody has read the surveys about balanced boards and balanced teams delivering better results, better culture, better retention – for many that is only a theoretical understanding. And the challenge is to translate that into practical action.'

Paul Polman (former CEO, Unilever; Impact Champion, HeforShe)

'Definitely there is enough data out there for a compelling business case . . . But if you say how widely it is understood . . . you have to look at the real facts out there and not get too emotional or judgemental about it, and the facts would say that it's not as widely understood as we would like it to be . . . And in fact no country in the world, as far as I can see with the work I do on the Sustainable Development Goals, has economic equality between the genders. So the reality is that it's in the heads of a lot of people but it's not in the heart, in my opinion.'

Cherie Blair CBE, QC (Founder and Chair, Omnia Strategy; founder, Cherie Blair Foundation for Women)

'I actually think sometimes that people acknowledge the business case but, given the lack of progress, it seems as though they read about the business case [and] they don't actually internalize it and find it compelling enough to make the changes that are needed.'

Carolyn Fairbairn (Director-General, CBI)

'The business case for gender balance is overwhelming and has only been increasing on the scale of importance for business. However, when the going gets tough, gender diversity can be one of the issues that slips down the list of priorities for a board.'

Brenda Trenowden (Global Chair, 30% Club)

'We often hear people saying, "Oh yes, you've got the business case / we've got the business case," but I think we do have to keep reiterating it because I think sometimes people say they get it and then they don't think about it. They don't think about the war for talent. They don't think about the fact that we need to avoid groupthink. They don't think about getting to know their consumers/customers better . . . It never hurts to keep reiterating all the reasons why diversity is good for business.'

Sarah Gordon (former Business Editor, *Financial Times*)

'If you understand intuitively that diversity . . . makes moral sense, I think you very easily get the point that it also makes commercial sense. I think that since so many companies and so many bosses are still doing extremely little, or the bare minimum, to genuinely increase diversity in their workforces and in their senior ranks, it's clear that it's not widely and truly understood by a lot of people.'

Melanie Richards (Deputy Chair, KPMG UK)

'I think it varies quite dramatically between businesses and I think the reason for that is, as much as there's a good body of evidence at a global and macro [level], I think it's good to try and get an individual business to get to that micro business case for themselves, which is the "why would they do it?" as much as the macro.'

Deborah Gilshan (Co-chair, 30% Club Investor Group)

'There are still a lot of business leaders who don't understand why this is important. I get frustrated that we keep getting asked about the business case for diversity when we were never asked for the business case and corresponding out-performance of companies with non-diverse boards.'

Joshua Graff (UK Country Manager and VP, LinkedIn Marketing Solutions, EMEA and LATAM)

'It's a survival issue over the next decade, and for the companies that can really effect change today, it will differentiate them in what is arguably a very competitive landscape at the moment.'

2 Five Snapshots of Global Gender Progress

| Figure 6: 5 Facts about Progress So Far

The Gender Pay Gap
The overall gender pay gap between male and female managers is over 26%

Top Performers
Iceland, Norway, Sweden and Finland top the list of the best countries for gender equality. They have all closed over 80% of their gender gaps

The 'Glass Pyramid'
Men are 40% more likely to get promoted, work in higher paid sectors and roles and are more likely to get (bigger) bonuses than women. In 2018, across 44 countries, only 5% of leadership appointments went to women

5 Facts about Progress So Far

Political Progress
Across 149 countries, only 11% have a female head of state and female ministers count for only 18% of the total

Women on Boards v. Women in Management
While 35% of non-executive directors are now female, the executive pipeline is stagnant with the number of female executive directors stuck at 9.7%

Views on the current state of gender balance may vary, but everyone agrees that progress is too slow. Julia Gillard, Australia's first female Prime Minister, who now heads up the Global Institute for Women's Leadership at King's College London, describes the progress as 'glacial'. She told me, 'Looking around the world, whether it's the percentage of women in parliament ... who lead big companies ... on boards, the percentage of news media leaders ... of women leading in technology, if we surveyed around the world, all of those statistics are under 30 per cent – many of them well under 30 per cent – and the corporate board statistic is under 20 per cent. So all of that's telling us that the size of the task to achieve gender balance and gender equality is a big one. And unfortunately, we can't take comfort from a galloping rate of change. While statistics are improving, they are improving slowly.'

This chapter gives a snapshot of progress through five lenses. Much of the data focuses on the UK (that's where CMI is based), but the patterns are repeated across the world.

1 Equal pay versus the gender pay gap
2 The 'glass pyramid' and its primary causes
3 Women on boards versus women in leadership and management
4 Political progress
5 Top performers

1. Equal pay versus the gender pay gap

Men and women are not paid equally. Women are paid less than men in every one of the 149 countries looked at by the World Economic Forum and in every broad-based survey on pay that I've seen.

It's important to distinguish between equal pay and the pay gap. They are two different things.

Equal pay is the rate of pay for doing the exact same job. The gender pay gap, meanwhile, is the overall amount women in a group (this could be an organization, profession, sector, country or even the world) are paid *on average versus men*.

On equal pay, many countries have laws making it illegal to pay men and women differently for doing the same job. In the UK, for example, it has been illegal since the Equal Pay Act of 1970.

That, however, doesn't mean it doesn't happen. Many women are paid far less than their male counterparts in the same job. If you're a female radio presenter or news editor at the BBC being paid a lot less than many of your male colleagues, that is not equal pay for the same job. This pay gap was exposed when the BBC published its salaries and has been criticized in an independent government review. Carrie Gracie, an international news editor, resigned over the issue when she learned she was being paid many thousands of pounds less, for doing similar work, than her male colleagues.

In the same vein, the actress Michelle Williams was paid $1,000 for reshooting scenes in the movie *All the Money in the World*, whereas the actor Mark Wahlberg got $1.5m. (He apparently donated the money to the Time's Up Hollywood campaign for gender equality.[1])

Many women have told me that they've discovered they're earning far less – often tens of thousands of pounds (or dollars) less – than their male colleagues for doing pretty much the same role. CMI and Ros Urwin of the *Sunday Times* analysed the pay of female CEOs, chairs and CFOs, and we found, to our surprise, that the six female FTSE CEOs were paid, on average, 55 per cent less than their male colleagues. The six female chairs were paid 77 per cent less, and the eleven CFOs were paid 46 per cent less.[2] The increased transparency around gender pay reporting, which I discuss below, will help to shed more light on this sensitive topic.

As for the gender pay gap, the main cause is the persistent under-representation of women in senior leadership and management positions – despite the fact that in many industries and professions there are more women in junior positions. Women, it seems, don't just face a 'glass ceiling', it's more like a 'glass pyramid' – with wider pay gaps for women the higher they reach.

2. The 'glass pyramid' and its primary causes

The 'glass pyramid' describes the shape of female leadership in organizations. And what that means is that there are many more women in the bottom quartile of organizations than at the top. As you progress to the upper quartile, the women slip off – hence the shape looks like a pyramid. By the time you get right to the top, men hold far more positions. And the higher

Figure 7: CMI 'Mind the Gender Pay Gap'

Source: CMI 'Mind the Gender Pay Gap' infographic, September 2018

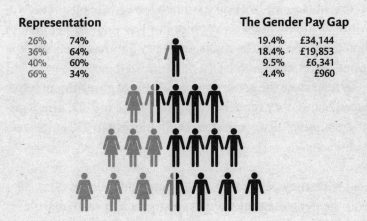

Representation		The Gender Pay Gap	
26%	74%	19.4%	£34,144
36%	64%	18.4%	£19,853
40%	60%	9.5%	£6,341
66%	34%	4.4%	£960

up the pyramid you go, the greater the gender pay gap between men and women. The absence of women in senior positions across all sectors is the main driver of the gender pay gap.

Let's take a closer look. As you can see, there are many women at the bottom of the pyramid – as more women attend university and graduate with better grades, so it's logical that they get a good job when they enter the workforce; in fact, women do represent two-thirds of junior managers. The pay gap in the bottom quartile of the pyramid is smaller – in this example it is 4 per cent between men and women.

By the time we reach the middle management, however, the situation has reversed. Some 60 per cent of managers are male, with 40 per cent female. And, tellingly, the pay gap has doubled to 10 per cent.

At the top of the pyramid, three-quarters of the roles are held by men, and the pay gap now averages 19 per cent – or £34,000-plus per year. This drives the overall pay gap beyond 26 per cent, meaning that, overall, male managers earn over 25 per cent more than their female counterparts at every level.

CMI has been monitoring the gender pay gap in the UK for many years. The sad truth is there's been little movement on this in the past five years; women have made up about two-thirds of junior managerial roles but less than 30 per cent of director roles; and the managerial pay gap has been stuck at about 26 per cent.[3]

To help close the gender pay gap, the UK government introduced mandatory gender pay gap reporting in 2017. This legislation requires all organizations with more than 250 employees to disclose:

- what they pay men versus women on average
- the percentage of women versus men in each quartile

- the percentage of men versus women receiving bonuses, and
- the 'bonus gap'.

CMI sat on the advisory committee for this and I was especially keen that companies report the information by quartile so they could see their own 'glass pyramids'. I was also very keen that the reporting include bonuses.

In April 2018, the month the gender pay gap information was due, I hosted a CMI event at Lloyd's of London. There were three male chairs and three female advocates there to discuss the findings. Each of the chairs was embarrassed by the stark reality of the data and wanted to work together to fix it. What I remember most from the occasion was the admission by Sir Terry Morgan, then Chairman of Crossrail, that he was nervous about this evening and had brought notes – something he wouldn't normally do. He did so because he knew the data would be so bad that it was 'indefensible'.

He was right. In a lot of cases, the findings were indefensible. The financial services sector, with the biggest pay gap, was particularly depressing. But all sectors need to up their game. I'll take a deeper look at several – including STEM (science, technology, engineering and maths) – later in this chapter.

As Dame Cilla Snowball, until recently Chair of the UK's largest advertising agency, commented, 'When I started in the advertising business in 1981 there were 11 per cent of ad agencies run by women, and now that's 31 per cent. So over that period there's been an impressive improvement. But if you calculate that forwards, I would be 96 before we achieve 50 per cent. And I'll be terrible when I'm 96!'

Alongside submitting gender pay gap information, companies

were asked to publish commentary about what they were planning to do about it. Sadly, not enough action plans were delivered alongside the pay gap reporting. What was revealed was a real lack of understanding of the issue. Asked about his company's gender pay gap of 68 per cent, the CEO of a retailer of women's clothing replied blithely, 'Oh, that's because all the women work in the shops and all the men work in management.' Another CEO commented that they had redoubled their efforts to recruit young women – on the basis that, over time, the pyramid would sort itself out. Again, as we've already seen, that is wishful thinking.

All this suggests we need more than transparency, we need transparency with teeth: a requirement to publish targets and action plans; and penalties and consequences for those who don't.[4]

There are three main causes of the 'glass pyramid'.

1 Men are more likely to get promoted than women.
2 Men work in higher-paid sectors and roles than women.
3 Men are more likely to get bonuses, and get bigger bonuses than women.

Let's look at each in turn and then some global examples. *Spoiler alert:* it's a similar picture everywhere!

The promotion gap

Men are more likely to get promoted than women. CMI looked at who got promoted over the previous twelve months. What we found was that men were 40 per cent more likely to get promoted than women. We call this the 'promotion gap' and it is perhaps the biggest cause of the 'glass pyramid', evidenced by a number of sources.

Figure 8: Women are Far Less Likely to be Promoted to Manager

Source: McKinsey & Company, 'Women in the Workplace 2018', October 2018, p. 9

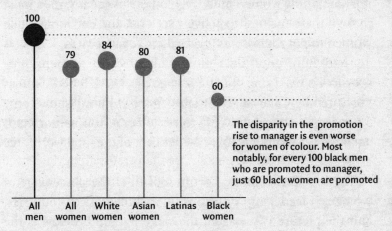

The disparity in the promotion rise to manager is even worse for women of colour. Most notably, for every 100 black men who are promoted to manager, just 60 black women are promoted

There are many reasons why women are less likely to progress than men. One of the most succinct summations I know comes from Professor Tom Schuller, who coined the idea of the 'Paula Principle'. This is a variation on the 'Peter Principle', which famously concluded that people are promoted to one level above their competence.

The Paula Principle concludes the exact opposite. It says that women are more likely to be promoted to one level *below* their competence. The reasons for this, as we will explore later, range from discrimination due to caring responsibilities and different work patterns, to lack of sponsorship or self-confidence, and different definitions of success. Together they contribute to what I call 'opt-out syndrome' and the stress caused by being an ambitious woman at odds with the predominantly male culture at work.[5]

Many women believe they should just get their head down and that one day someone will come along, recognize all their hard work, and promote them – putting a metaphorical crown on their head. There's even a name for this – 'tiara syndrome', coined by American psychologists Frohlinger and Kolb – and it is something women must overcome. But equally, men must make it their business to actively seek out and encourage such women to put themselves forward for advancement.

Thankfully, good data on the obstacles to women's progression is emerging. Take, for example, the US S&P 500, as measured by Catalyst. Their latest 'glass pyramid' shows only 5 per cent of women in CEO roles; 26 per cent in senior management positions; and over 44 per cent of the total workforce as female.[6]

The World Economic Forum looked at the percentage of women in leadership positions in a whole host of countries, and the picture is yet again the same pyramid. Below is the graph, distilled from the WEF 2017 data.[7]

And work from McKinsey, focused on corporate America, has shown exactly the same pattern. In their 2018 'Women in

Figure 9: Women are Under-represented at Every Level in the Corporate Pipeline'

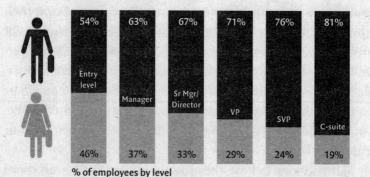

% of employees by level

the Workplace' report, they found that for every 100 men promoted only 79 women were.[8]

The situation is even worse for ethnic minorities, and especially for women of colour. They comprised 17 per cent of the entry-level workforce but only 3 per cent of the C-suite. We will look at some of the issues and drivers for better ethnic balance in Chapters 3 and 4. Figure 8 summarizes promotion rates for men versus women.

Research has also highlighted the 'one and done' theory. The number of businesses with at least one female in senior leadership advanced globally in 2018 versus 2017 from 66 per cent to 75 per cent. But at the same time, the overall percentage of roles held by senior women declined from 25 per cent to 24 per cent according to Grant Thornton, authors of the report.[9] This could be indicating a 'tick box' or tokenistic approach to gender diversity – the appointment of a single woman on an otherwise all-male team – rather than genuine efforts to fix the problem and create balance.[10] The UK's Hampton-Alexander Review has coined the phrase 'one and done' to describe companies that appoint one woman to the board or leadership team and then assume their job is done.[11]

More and more researchers are starting to track the critical mass of 30 per cent women on an executive team or board. There is still much work needed to hit this number. Women still only account for about 25 per cent of all senior roles globally; they represent 22 per cent of all executive teams in the Americas, 15 per cent in Europe and 4 per cent in Asia.[12] The reality is that leadership at the top remains more or less stagnant. Egon Zehnder, the C-suite search firm, analysed the situation in top public companies in 44 countries and found that a meagre 5 per cent of leadership appointments went to women in 2018. And the Hampton-Alexander Review, which analysed the executive pipeline in the FTSE 350, concluded that the appointment rate for women to executive positions would need to increase significantly – from about one-third to just under half – if they were to reach the target of 33 per cent female executive committee members in the FTSE 100 by 2020.[13]

So the early evidence suggests that transparency alone without teeth – in the form of clear targets and action plans, pressure and consequences – isn't enough to move the needle. According to the *Financial Times*, one year on from mandatory gender pay gap reporting in the UK, the median pay gap so far has shifted only marginally, from 11.8 per cent to 11.4 per cent.[14]

| Table 1: Gender Pay Gap Data

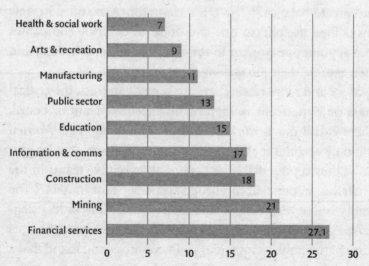

Data compiled by Louis Goddard, *Sunday Times*

Sectors and roles

The lack of female leaders is compounded by the fact that women are concentrated in lower-paid sectors, while men work in higher-paid sectors and roles. At CMI we analysed the gender pay gap by sector and found that men were much more likely to hold senior positions in well-paid industries such as IT and financial services, while women hold positions in the lower-paid healthcare, not-for-profit and public sectors. I call this the 'pink collar' effect, and the gender pay gap data from the UK confirms that the gap is widest in the financial services sector and smallest in the health sector.

You are never too late to take action to understand – and fix – your gender pay gap. Here's an example of a programme that's just started.

HSBC

HSBC had the largest pay gap of any big company in Britain in 2018 – men are paid on average 59 per cent more than women[15] – but Group Chief Operating Officer Andy Maguire is determined to address this. 'It's not about fixing the ethnic minorities or women, it's about fixing the boys that are here . . . I need people who can form teams, who have empathy, who can listen . . . attributes not normally associated with the male half of the species . . . These are the things that are most important,' he told Professor Susan Vinnicombe,

Professor of Women and Leadership at Cranfield School of Management, who helped HSBC design the programme. HSBC's aim is that 50 per cent of new appointments should be women, and male buy-in is essential. An 'Inclusive Talent Management' template helped improve career movement for women. They introduced strategic career-planning workshops and developed a female talent pool from which selectors could shortlist candidates for career progression.

To assist those responsible for hiring, performance management and promotion, they adopted 'conscious decision-making' to focus on what could be done to avoid preconceived judgements (initially by senior leaders but then rolled out across HSBC). The executive committee became engaged in the programme as sponsors, championing individuals. This initiative grew to become a reciprocal mentoring scheme. Maguire is involving the line managers who were most receptive to change. It's too early to measure results – but let's hope he succeeds.[16]

Job roles are an important factor in preventing women from reaching leadership positions. Women tend to occupy less high-profile 'staff roles' such as human resources, marketing and communications, whereas men take up the more visible and highly paid 'line' roles with revenue and profit responsibility. This drives the differences in bonuses between male and female leaders. With a nice turn of phrase, Brenda Trenowden, Global Chair of the 30% Club, says we need to 'hack into the path to the top and change it so there isn't just one route'. Many experts agree with her.

In 2018 the World Economic Forum teamed up with LinkedIn to look at women's progress by sector. In every one, women made up less than 50 per cent of the leadership. The lowest percentage of female leaders was found in finance, software, mining, energy and manufacturing – and in the last three the percentage of women leaders globally was less than 20 per cent. McKinsey did in-depth research into the US financial services market in September 2018 and found that while the number of women and men in the entry-level roles was roughly the same, the men outnumbered the women by more than four times once they reached the C-suite: 81 per cent versus 19 per cent.[17] In all twelve sectors McKinsey looked at, the proportion of women leaders increased by only 2 per cent across a ten-year period.

CASE STUDY

Women in STEM

The World Economic Forum has also looked at the under-representation of women relative to the talent pool. They looked at the percentage of women in a given field relative to the number of female members of LinkedIn that had a degree in a given subject area. Again, they found women over-represented in lower-paying professions such as education, not-for-profit and healthcare; and least represented in the STEM fields such as software, IT, energy and engineering.

The STEM problem is an extreme example of gender inequality, and it has many causes. In the UK only 14 per cent of STEM workers are female; in the USA, the figure is 16 per cent; in Australia, the figure is also 16 per cent. In 2016, across the European Union, women accounted for well below 30 per cent of graduates in engineering and only 32 per cent of high-tech sector employees.[18] And yet, these are the jobs that are growing most rapidly in the economy as a whole.[19] This is an important problem to solve, as skills shortages are particularly acute in this area – we need an estimated 900,000 engineers in the UK alone, and yet we are the country with the lowest percentage of women in STEM careers in Europe.

Women drop out from STEM careers at every stage, including high school. Too few girls take physics at school and, of those who do well, only one in five remain in the sector – compared to 50 per cent of boys. Tackling this issue will only become more important, given advances in technology.

Unlike other areas such as law, where women now make up the majority of students in many countries, there are still far too few women at the beginning of the pipeline. In the USA, for example, there are almost six times as many white, male computer science undergraduates compared with women, black people and other ethnic groups. Only 18 per cent of females are engineers, although the majority of US undergraduates are women.[20]

Even if women do progress in these sectors, they find few role models and a new set of obstacles.[21] One study concluded that female developers aged 35-plus were 3.5 times more likely to be 'stuck' in junior roles versus their male counterparts.[22]

Big Tech has come under fire for its macho 'brogrammer' culture. In 2018, Google faced a class action lawsuit affecting more than 8,000 women who allege that women are paid less than men for the same jobs, and are siphoned off into lower-paying positions. Three-quarters of all leadership roles in this big tech company are held by men.[23] This ratio exists across Silicon Valley and yet – *sigh* – over 90 per cent of employees still think diversity isn't an issue.[24]

Some companies are trying to break the mould. The finance and HR software company Workday now has six women in the C-Suite, and holds third place in the Great Place to Work standings. At a recent CMI event, an engineering boss described how he had pioneered efforts to attract female apprentices into his sector by insisting that one female apprentice be appointed for every male apprentice.

Progress made does not equate to progress sustained. Without constant pressure to progress, pioneers drop back.

Dame Stephanie Shirley, founder, Sopra Steria

Back to the future: Tech pioneer Dame Stephanie Shirley's experience shows the importance of staying vigilant to avoid reverting to old habits.

Sopra Steria was a pioneer in pushing gender balance. The company's founder, Dame Stephanie Shirley, came to the UK from Germany as part of the *Kindertransport* scheme just before the Second World War. From a very early age, Shirley learned how to be resilient and adapt to change.

These experiences served her well when she embarked upon her career in the financial services and computing industries. In 1962 she started Sopra Steria. This was a time when women were not allowed to work in the Stock Exchange, to drive a bus, to fly an aeroplane, or even to open a bank account without their husband's permission.

Steve – she gave herself the nickname to hide her female identity – battled sexism. Most people thought it ridiculous that a woman might want to run a serious company. She laughs at the memory. She coined the term 'flat heads' for ambitious women like her who were regularly patted and patronized.

Steve pushed on, motivated to inspire other women. Sopra Steria adopted a 'Jobs for Women' policy from the start: 297 of the first 300 employees were female!

From the earliest days, Steve was a champion of flexible working and other policies that enabled women to focus on their career as well as their home life. Productivity soared, and her female programmers programmed the black box for the supersonic Concorde from the comfort of their own homes. They also wrote software that could be used for underwater weapons research and stock control. Sopra's workplace standards were eventually adopted by NATO and the Department of Health. In 1975, the Sex Discrimination Act was passed and Sopra's positive discrimination ended. The gender ratio stabilized at 60/40, female:male.

Today, Sopra Steria is a very different company to the one Stephanie created. She says, 'It looks pretty [much] like any other corporate, and the gender pay gap shows the senior positions [are] mainly held by men.' Female employees' hourly rate of pay is 26 per cent lower than the men's. In terms of the 'glass pyramid', 57 per cent of the lowest-paid employees in Sopra Steria are women; only 17.7 per cent of the highest-paid are women. Stephanie attributes some of this to the organization's growth: many of Sopra Steria's acquisitions have been of predominantly male organizations. 'It is just a depressing story,' she says today.

It is all too easy for organizations to revert to gender imbalance. Whatever initiatives your organization has put in place to improve the state of the 'glass pyramid' and the gender pay gap, remember that only vigilance will prevent their demise.

Salaries and bonuses

Men are more likely to get bonuses, and to get bigger bonuses than women. CMI has looked at relative bonus payments for men versus women, and the results are shocking. In 2018, we found that male CEO bonuses were 83 per cent higher than women's – £83,230 versus £14,945 on average. Or, to put it another way, nearly six times that of women! Men also got bigger perks. And overall, more men than women got bonuses – at senior levels, 54 per cent of men received a bonus compared to just 38 per cent of women.

That's why we pushed hard for bonus payments to be included in the UK government's gender reporting regulations so that you could compare the average bonus gaps between men and women. These gaps remain significant, particularly in sectors such as financial services, where women's bonuses are often half those of their male counterparts.

In fact, in the FTSE 100 it is very much the bonuses, share awards and other perks that drive the differences in pay, rather than base salaries. The base salaries of female CEOs, for example, are only 12 per cent lower than the salaries of male CEOs. The gap between male and female bonuses and perks, however, was well over 50 per cent. Ouch!

3. Women on boards versus women in leadership and management

There is one area where a huge amount of effort and progress has been made in the past decade, and that is women on boards.

According to MSCI, an investment services firm which regularly monitors the percentage of women on boards across 4,200 companies globally, 2018 saw the percentage of women on boards increase to 17.9 per cent – up from 15.8 per cent in 2016. The best performers are in developed Western markets – gains were made in the UK, USA and France. Progress was slowest in East Asian countries.

Despite this progress, MSCI estimates that it will be at least 2029 before the companies in their index achieve an average of 30 per cent women on their boards; more than one-fifth of the companies they monitor still have all-male boards. They also note that the rate of change is slowing. In terms of sectors, IT has performed worst, while utilities and financial firms performed best.[25]

In the UK a number of initiatives have really pushed for women on boards in the past years: the Cranfield FTSE 100 report, the 30% Club and the Davies Review are just three. They have worked closely together across business, government and the media. The 30 per cent target was set because this is widely regarded as the 'tipping point' for encouraging more cultural diversity. The goal of having 30 per cent women on boards in the FTSE 100 was actually achieved in September 2018 and shows just how much progress can be made through joined-up, concerted efforts; in 2010 the comparable figure was only 12.5 per cent.

The 30% Club and Hampton-Alexander have now turned

their attention to getting more women into the so-called 'executive pipeline' – people in the top leadership and management roles who actually run the companies day by day. Because while there are currently 30.2 per cent female directors on FTSE 100 boards, and 24.9 per cent across the FTSE 250, the executive pipeline has been pretty stagnant, or is going backwards.

I believe that an unintended consequence of increasing women's presence on boards first has been to slow progress in management and leadership positions. Many male senior leaders, including chairmen, think they've addressed the 'women on boards issue'. A recent study in the USA found that the top companies for diverse boards were much less likely to have similar diversity on their executive committees.[26] As a FTSE chairman remarked to me, 'I'm tired of talking about this gender thing. It's time to talk about promoting the right talent.' This gender fatigue and 'we've ticked that box, can we move on now?' attitude isn't helpful and is a major cause of the current inertia.

4. Political progress

Women are still dramatically under-represented in the political arena. Of the four areas it examined, the World Economic Forum found the gap here to be the largest – 23 per cent. Only 17 out of the 149 countries they looked at had female heads of state, while female ministers accounted for 18 per cent of the total and 24 per cent of parliamentarians.[27]

Women need to enter politics so they can shape the social, economic and political agendas that encourage gender balance. Getting more women to participate in the political arena is part of the solution to achieving gender balance in other organizations. The World Economic Forum has found a correlation between the highest permanent countries on the political index and economic participation.[28]

And yet, as I heard recently from former Australian Prime Minister Julia Gillard and current Labour MP Jess Phillips, female politicians can suffer vile abuse. In both their cases, these have included death and rape threats, and, in Jess's case, being sent pictures of her children hanging. This comes on top of acts of bullying and discrimination and 'toxic culture' that an independent inquiry into parliamentary culture in the UK recently outed.

The report concluded that the acts of bullying and harassment had an obvious gender dimension.[29] Julia Gillard famously spoke out against misogyny in a speech in Australia's Parliament and has since gone on to chair the Global Institute for Women's Leadership at King's College London. Gillard told me, 'I think a big barrier to change is the failure of political parties to take this seriously. When political parties do take gender equality seriously, they are capable of bringing a relatively quick rate of change . . . I look at my own political party in Australia . . . which decided they would have an affirmative action target and deliberately reach out to women and try to generate more women candidates. That's taken us from 14 per cent of our parliamentarians in our national parliament being women in the 1990s to very nearly 50 per cent now.'

The French presidency

Ségolène Royal was the French Socialist Party's presidential candidate in 2007. In an interview, Ms Royal recounts the sexism she uncovered within her own party and, worse, from her own husband.

When Royal announced she would be running in the presidential election, Laurent Fabius, former French Prime Minister, exclaimed, 'But who's going to look after the children?' In fact, the sexism had begun long before her presidential campaign. Royal has talked of being asked to remove her clothes by a backbencher in Parliament; being asked to talk about a 'trifling matter' while serving as a junior education minister; and having to bring a civil servant before a disciplinary hearing for telling junior female colleagues to be seated at a meeting according to their breast size.[30]

There are some encouraging signs. In the US mid-term elections in 2018 a record number of women – 102 in total – were elected to Congress (90 per cent are in the Democratic party). This is up from only 23 in 1987. This progress is a backlash against President Trump's policies and behaviours. Still, about six in ten women think that America hasn't gone far enough when it comes to gender equality, compared with four in ten men.[31]

5. Top performers

Benchmarking is creating new ways of promoting and sharing transparency, and signposting progress. Many new indices are emerging, while established ones are gaining authority. As Peter Grauer, Chairman of Bloomberg (creator of the Gender-Equality Index, or GEI), says, 'Bloomberg's standardized gender reporting framework serves as an underlying tool to guide disclosure, allowing companies to measure and manage gender equality . . . It also provides these leading organizations an opportunity to inspire each other and develop best practices.'[32]

Overall best for gender balance

The World Economic Forum has for a number of years listed the top ten countries for overall gender equality. The 2018 list shows a familiar group: Iceland, Norway, Sweden, Finland (all have closed over 80 per cent of their gap), followed by Nicaragua, Rwanda, New Zealand, the Philippines, Ireland and Namibia.

Iceland has been ranked by the World Economic Forum as the best country in the world for gender equality for the past nine years running. This has been achieved with immense backing from the Icelandic government which, in 2018, made it illegal to pay women less than men. The aim is to eradicate the gender pay gap by 2022.

Under the new legislation, organizations with more than 25 employees will be required to obtain government certification demonstrating their pay equality. Companies who don't comply will face fines. The new law received support from both the centre-right coalition government and the opposition in Parliament (where, it should be noted, nearly 50 per cent of the lawmakers are women).[33]

Women on boards

There is no doubt that much progress has been made in getting women on boards since 2010, albeit starting from a very low base. Catalyst produced their snapshot in December 2018. It is worth noting that most of the countries in the list have quota requirements and/or penalties for not hitting targets.

Catalyst also classified their countries by the willingness to tackle the issue as identified by the 30% Club leaders. Of the

25 champion countries, 12 had quotas; 13 did not. Of the 13 countries with 30 per cent or more women on boards, however, all but one – Sweden – had quotas operating. Still, some of the most successful examples – Australia and the UK – have avoided this, relying instead on voluntary public–private partnerships and pressure from other stakeholders. I will look at voluntary efforts versus quotas in Chapter 4.

Based on an analysis of 4,000 mid-market companies, Grant Thornton found that the percentage of women in senior management roles ranges from a high of 36 per cent in Eastern Europe to a low of 21 per cent in North America – a finding which may surprise some.[34]

Table 2: Women's Global Representation on Boards, 2010–2017

Source: Catalyst, 'Quick Take: Women on Corporate Boards', 21 December 2018

Country	% Women Director-ships, 2017	% Women Director-ships, 2010	% with Three or More WOB, 2017	% with One or More WOB, 2017	% with Zero WOB, 2017	Quota and Year Introduced
Australia	28.7	10.2	48.5	95.6	4.4	No
Canada	25.8	12.9	57.9	95.8	4.2	Pending
Finland	33.7	24.2	75.0	100.0	0.0	Yes, 2008
France	40.8	12.7	100.0	100.0	0.0	Yes, 2010
Germany	20.9	10.7	80.0	94.5	5.5	Yes, 2015
India	13.8	4.5	13.2	93.4	6.6	Yes, 2013
Italy	35.8	3.6	100.0	100.0	0.0	Yes, 2011
Japan	5.3	0.9	0.6	47.7	52.3	No
Netherlands	22.1	13.9	57.1	96.4	3.6	Yes, 2013
Switzerland	21.3	9.2	35.0	97.5	2.5	Yes
UK	26.8	8.9	64.3	100.0	0.0	No
US	21.7	12.3	39.2	97.4	2.6	No

Top companies for management and boards
So which are the best-performing companies? An investment company called Equileap has started publishing its list of the top 200 companies according to:

- the number of women on the board and in executive and senior roles
- policies towards achieving gender balance, and
- career progression opportunities.

Equileap's top ten might surprise you:

1 General Motors
2 L'Oréal
3 Kering
4 Merck
5 Starhub
6 Tele2
7 Westpac
8 National Australia Bank
9 Swedbank
10 JP Morgan Chase
11 Diageo (the best UK performer that deserves a mention!)[35]

Equileap also looked at the percentage of eligible companies per country that were included in the top 200 ranking. Not surprisingly, Norway topped the list.

New ways of creating and sharing transparency are emerging. Bloomberg's global Gender-Equality Index (GEI), for example, includes 230 $1billion-plus public companies from 13 countries.

Table 3: Company Performance by Country

Source: Equileap, Gender Equality Global Report and Ranking, 2018 Edition, p. 15

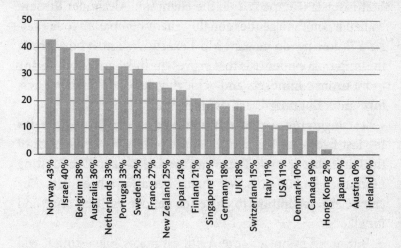

They achieved a 40 per cent increase in the number of female executives over the past five years – far ahead of the average. Still, their average gender pay gap in 2019 was 20 per cent.[36]

In summary

Despite all the best intentions and many inspirational initiatives, progress towards gender balance is either flatlining or, worse, going backwards. This is a tragedy. All the experts I've spoken to say that we need to inject urgency into public and private efforts, policy and measurement.

As Professor Susan Vinnicombe, founder of Cranfield's International Centre for Women Leaders, says, 'The female talent pipeline is busy going nowhere.' Even the usually optimistic

Helena Morrissey, founder of the 30% Club, is angry about the absence of momentum in the executive pipeline.

As Dominic Barton, Global Managing Partner Emeritus at McKinsey & Company, told the Hampton-Alexander Review, 'When it comes to gender equality, many companies today suffer a "knowing–doing gap". Most executives know how strong the empirical evidence is that proves the link between fostering more diverse mindsets and achieving superior financial performance. But progress is still too slow.'[37]

It's staggering we haven't achieved more. Every year for the last five years I've spoken at the head girls' conference of the Girl's Day Schools Trust – a group of 23 schools educating more than 24,000 girls. My theme has always been that they can be the generation to close the gender pay gap once and for all.

But now I'm not so sure. With estimates suggesting it will take another 60 to 100 years to achieve gender parity, many of those 17-year-olds won't be around.

So why is this such a stubborn and persistent issue? There are many reasons, both rational and behavioural, intentional and unintentional, societal, political, cultural and historical. There is much inertia at an organizational and individual level. There is also a bit of a backlash, or 'gender fatigue', or 'what about me?' from many men – and some unhelpful behaviour from women themselves.

In the next chapter, we'll look at why, despite overwhelming evidence that gender balance is good for business and the economy, we aren't better at making it happen faster.

What Other Experts Say

How would you describe the rate of progress on gender balance?

Paul Polman (former CEO, Unilever; Impact Champion, HeforShe)

'It's going in the wrong direction . . . There is a mismatch be-tween behaviour and belief, and heart and head, if you [can] call it that way, because the direction we are going and the numbers don't add up to what the economic case would say. And that's obviously where the challenge is.'

Carolyn Fairbairn (Director-General, CBI)

'The FTSE 350 currently has fifteen female CEOs but that number has declined, not increased, over the last three years. Three years ago, FTSE 350 companies had eighteen CEOS. We are not making the progress we need to turn the dial. We have made some progress in many ways, but as the above statistic highlights, we're not yet on a relentless march forward.'

Sir Philip Hampton (Chair, Hampton-Alexander Review)

'There's a clear pattern, that the higher you go in the executive structure the more likely it is that you'll still see the number of female CEOs is very low. It's actually gone back a bit. Female CFOs and the routine executive slots on boards are similarly low. Female chairs are higher but still very low overall. All of these are disappointing figures . . . it's not clear why these very top roles, which will also be the top role models, remain so decisively male.'

Sam Smethers (CEO, Fawcett Society)

'I think we've seen very slow progress and that's disappointing. But I think it is partly because we've only relatively recently understood why it's important and taken any action to do something about it. And then we're not really very good at it yet in translating that into practice for employers and, you know, having an action plan in place and a sense of direction about it . . . and then the other thing still very slow to change . . . is the lack of women at the top and the congregation of women at the bottom, which is really a kind of segregation in the labour market [which] is still incredibly marked . . . you've got every sector basically dominated by men. It is quite shocking when you step back and look at it. I think it shows that we've still got a huge distance to travel before we start to achieve equality.'

Ivan Menezes (CEO, Diageo)

'The change we need to make won't happen overnight but it will happen with the right level of ambition and action. And I hope that by sharing our experience and by working together we can achieve the progress we all aspire to that little bit faster.'

Sarah Gordon (former Business Editor, *Financial Times*)

'Obviously there has been progress but the progress has been terribly slow . . . Gloria Steinem says that women are the only group that gets more radical with age, and one of the reasons that we do is because the fact that things are changing so slowly becomes more and more apparent. I don't really believe that women coming into the workforce in most countries have more opportunities than I had over thirty years ago when I joined the workforce.'

Baroness Mary Goudie (Co-founder, 30% Club)

'I feel we have made good progress but we have to ensure we don't go back at any point. So we have to keep the pressure on.'

3   The Top Five Pitfalls Preventing Gender Balance

| **Figure 10: 5 Pitfalls Preventing Gender Balance**

Culture – Broken Windows

80% of women have seen inappropriate behaviour or remarks based on gender, and the same number have been prevented from expressing their views at work

Recruitment, Training and Reward Practices Gone Wrong

Women are more likely to receive critical feedback based on gender.
Using gender-neutral descriptors in recruitment ads achieves a 40% broader pool of applicants

Lack of Networking and Sponsorship

Only 1 in 10 managers have seen sponsorship used to support junior female managers, and only 6% of managers have been sponsored themselves

5 Pitfalls Preventing Gender Balance

The Confidence Gap

If a woman sees 10 attributes listed for a job and she meets 9, she'll stress about the one she doesn't meet. If a man meets 6 out of 10, he'll conclude he's clearly the best candidate

The Motherhood Penalty, Fatherhood Bonus and Flexible Working Stigma

65% of mothers say that having children negatively impacted their career. While mothers on average earn 4% less per child, fathers' pay actually increases by 6% per child

'Unconscious bias is everywhere.'
– Iris Bohnet, *What Works*

In January 2018, CMI published 'A Blueprint for Balance', a major study designed to shine the spotlight on practices that work in achieving gender parity. As part of that work we interviewed more than 850 managers and conducted 70 in-depth interviews and best-practice conversations. We asked people to score their company's practices on gender balance using the net promoter score (NPS).

What we found was illuminating (though probably unsurprising). People score their companies worst for the things that are hardest to fix: culture and mentoring and sponsorship came out at the bottom. On the more process-oriented solutions, people scored their organizations slightly better. And only one metric had a positive score – recruitment practices. All the others came out negative. And the most positive score was only 2 out of 100, with the other scores 0 or even as poor as –39.

Drawing on CMI's research, as well as many experts and

Table 4: How Far Do Your Organization's Practices Support Gender Balance?

Source: CMI Women, 'A Blueprint for Balance' report, January 2018, p. 5

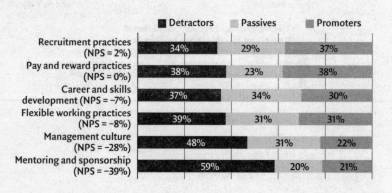

	Detractors	Passives	Promoters
Recruitment practices (NPS = 2%)	34%	29%	37%
Pay and reward practices (NPS = 0%)	38%	23%	38%
Career and skills development (NPS = –7%)	37%	34%	30%
Flexible working practices (NPS = –8%)	39%	31%	31%
Management culture (NPS = –28%)	48%	31%	22%
Mentoring and sponsorship (NPS = –39%)	59%	20%	21%

thought leaders, I think the top five pitfalls preventing gender balance are:

1 Culture
2 Lack of networking and sponsorship opportunities
3 Flexible and part-time working stigma: 'the parent (motherhood) trap'
4 Recruitment, and talent and reward practices
5 The confidence gap

1. Culture

'Broken windows' behaviours

The former New York City Mayor Rudy Giuliani famously believed that the trick to reducing serious offences – armed robbery, rape, murder – was to crack down and prevent the more minor transgressions such as hopping subway turnstiles or breaking windows.

The same, I believe, holds true for gender balance. If you tolerate the little incivilities, then you contribute to a culture where it's still okay to get away with the bigger things such as pay disparity, lack of promotion opportunities, and even sexual harassment.

The most common 'broken windows' behaviours (McKinsey dubs them 'micro-aggressions') are inappropriate remarks. This kind of thing:

- 'Sarah just had a baby, she won't be as committed so we can't give her that job.'
- 'Amanda is so abrasive, she really needs to watch her tone.'

- 'Oh hello, nurse, is the doctor here?' (Said to a young female consultant who had just examined a patient, wearing a doctor's uniform and stethoscope and who had introduced herself as the doctor.)

Some of these remarks are even more blatant: the experienced chairman who boasted of his three 'stunning' female directors; the trader who congratulated his sole female colleague on her bonus. 'Now you can go get a boob job,' he shouted.

Women can fall into the same patterns of behaviour. One senior finance woman in a well-known tech company felt her promotion was long overdue. Summoning her courage, she set up an appointment with her boss, listed her accomplishments and asked for the promotion. Her boss, also a woman, looked at her and said, 'You're being very aggressive in asking for that promotion, aren't you?' The finance professional held her gaze and calmly replied, 'Would you have said that to me if I were a man?' She got her promotion.

'Call it out, challenge it, change it' is the mantra we've developed at CMI to deal with such 'broken windows' behaviours – however light-hearted or unintentional they may seem.

Many 'broken windows behaviours' involve jumping to conclusions or adopting stereotypical roles. This could be:

- assuming that women will take minutes
- speaking over women in meetings ('manterrupting')
- not giving women credit for their ideas ('Brilliant idea, John!' when in fact it was Jane who first tabled it five minutes ago)
- launching into pedantic explanations ('mansplaining'), or

Table 5: Many Women Face Micro-aggressions, and These Encounters Add Up

Source: McKinsey & Company, 'Women in the Workplace 2018', October 2018, p. 19

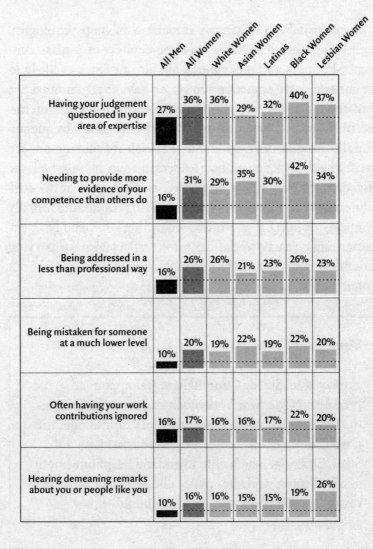

	All Men	All Women	White Women	Asian Women	Latinas	Black Women	Lesbian Women
Having your judgement questioned in your area of expertise	27%	36%	36%	29%	32%	40%	37%
Needing to provide more evidence of your competence than others do	16%	31%	29%	35%	30%	42%	34%
Being addressed in a less than professional way	16%	26%	26%	21%	23%	26%	23%
Being mistaken for someone at a much lower level	10%	20%	19%	22%	19%	22%	20%
Often having your work contributions ignored	16%	17%	16%	16%	17%	22%	20%
Hearing demeaning remarks about you or people like you	10%	16%	16%	15%	15%	19%	26%

- casually excluding women with endless sports banter ('Ugh,' one woman told me, 'if I have to listen to one more round of rugby results for the first ten minutes of every meeting, I'll go mad').

Such incivilities negatively impact women's psychological well-being and perpetuate their perception of a glass ceiling.[1] McKinsey reckons women are almost twice as likely to be mistaken for someone junior, or have their competence questioned, as men – with the figures much higher for minority women. Women in technology companies frequently cite the 'brogrammer' culture as a reason for moving on. 'It's great when you get passionate leaders up in front,' says Melanie Richards, Deputy Chair of KPMG and member of the 30% Club and the Hampton-Alexander Steering Group, 'but actually it means nothing if the micro-behaviours somebody is experiencing on a day-to-day basis don't reflect what we're trying to achieve. Which is why it's so important that we think about culture, as much as targets.'

Step up at Stock Exchange?

In May 2018, Stacey Cunningham was appointed president of the New York Stock Exchange, becoming the first woman in its 226-year history ever to hold this post. Cunningham recounts when she first joined the Stock Exchange, she had to use an old telephone booth as a bathroom while her male colleagues had luxurious restrooms complete with couches and full-time attendants.

Harassment

Left unchecked, these everyday transgressions contribute to a culture that views more serious discrimination, including sexual harassment, as somehow 'okay', as 'locker room banter'.

Sexual harassment also takes place in supposedly modern, progressive companies. This is, arguably, even more troubling.

At Google, a top employee received a $90m dollar payout even after he had been accused of sexual harassment. The disclosure prompted a walkout globally by some 20,000 Google employees, many of whom shared their own experiences of sexual harassment at work.[2] Similarly, WeWork, an office-sharing company that's hailed as the workplace of the future (and enjoys a $20bn valuation), faced allegations of promoting a frat boy culture where women were routinely groped and harassed, often at office party events that women were explicitly encouraged to attend.[3]

In many of these cases, employees have been asked to sign NDAs – legally binding non-disclosure agreements that prohibit them from coming forward with the allegations of harassment and discrimination. And in Australia, sex discrimination commissioner Kate Jenkins says that, for many women, the repercussions of reporting sexual harassment have been worse than the discrimination itself.[4] In the UK Sir Philip Hampton commented on this at the Hampton-Alexander Review launch in 2018: 'It's actually quite difficult as a victim to come forward because you think your career may be prejudiced. It is the responsibility of companies to have cultures and procedures that promote safe working environments and allow the ability to speak up.'

There are glimmers of hope. The Google walkout prompted the tech giant's CEO Sundar Pichai to publicly condemn the incidents and, more importantly, to alter company policy.

Apathy, denial and antipathy

> *'It feels like a revolution and, like all revolutions, it's*
> *facing a backlash.'*
> – Miriam González Durántez (Hampton-Alexander
> Review launch, 2018)

For all the talk about gender equality at work, only one in four managers visibly champions gender initiatives, according to CMI's research. Apathy, denial and antipathy are more common than action.

Part of the problem is that senior leadership isn't always regarded as sincere. Unless gender initiatives are believed in and understood, implemented and measured at every level of an organization, they're unlikely to progress and can be outright resented in the middle layers of a company. A Financial Reporting Council study found that while 97 per cent of the FTSE 350 have diversity plans, only 15 per cent report on their progress with them.[5] As one senior woman in a company that has set a target confided, most men were ignoring it as there were no consequences for doing so.[6] Another senior male executive told me, 'I've been successful doing what I am doing for over thirty years. Why should I bother to change now?'

The problem is, executives who don't want to change are often overly dismissive of those who do. A female managing director in financial services recalled a question put to her by her own boss about the diversity and inclusion council she'd instigated. 'How is that thing going?' he asked. 'That thing you do? What's that thing you're on? There's zero interest.'

In some companies, men are openly complaining that their chances are being scuppered because of giving opportunities to women. A group of white, male advertising executives accused J. Walter Thompson (JWT) of discrimination after being made redundant. The accusations came after the (female) creative director announced a diversity drive and promised to obliterate the 'Knightsbridge boys' club' after the agency revealed a median gender pay gap of 44.7 per cent in favour of men.[7]

I was shocked when speaking to a group of high-powered chairmen about the lack of progress on gender balance, only to be met by folded arms and accusations of 'politicizing' the data. Finally one looked at me and said he was sick to death of talking about gender, it had been done. It was time to move on.

The facts state otherwise.

The last cultural behaviour that gets in the way comes from women themselves. We've all seen very accomplished, impeccably dressed female executives who have reached great heights as CEOs or chairs. When they speak on a podium and, inevitably, are asked what barriers they faced as they ascended the ladder, they say convincingly that they have never felt held back because of their gender.

I would submit to you that they are not telling the whole truth. Sadly, many successful women still feel compelled to hide their own messy and often fraught journeys to the top. Once they leave the podium and are in an informal setting, they are often much more open about the struggles they have faced.[8]

Some women achieve their position by becoming an 'honorary man'. These women believe that others need to toughen up and go through the same rite of passage. They're often accused of actively not helping other women. This is known as 'Queen Bee syndrome'. One world-class professional woman once told me how unhelpful her female boss had been regarding her aspirations to follow in her footsteps. 'Since she'd had to tough it out, she felt I had to do the same thing.' The worry, says Andy Woodfield, Chief Marketing and Sales Officer at PwC, is that some women feel they must be 'more like a man than a man'.

A former colleague of mine, now the most senior woman in a global company, openly counsels other women: 'Don't do it like I did it, all sharp-suited and power-shouldered. Do it differently. Do you.'

2. Lack of networking and sponsorship opportunities

Almost every successful woman I know has had a male sponsor at some point in her career. But right now, sponsorship isn't as pervasive as it should be. Only one in ten managers in CMI's research have used sponsorship to support junior female managers, and only 6 per cent of managers have been sponsored themselves. Any inspirational examples that do exist lack visibility.[9]

Why is sponsorship not more widespread?
Many opportunities for informal sponsorship and networking occur in settings that exclude women. Men will often socialize after work in the pub or engage in sports activities; many women, however, need to get home for caring responsibilities. Women with partners are more than five times as likely to do the majority of childcare, and so they often miss out on vital, informal networking as a result.

Another reason more women aren't sponsored – described by Iris Bohnet and other experts – is that we're all more comfortable sponsoring people who look, dress and act like us. The unfortunate consequence of there being more men in senior leadership roles is that there are fewer women who get access to sponsorship. Men also feel less comfortable sponsoring women outside a formal structured programme.

Sponsorship versus mentoring (and reverse mentoring)

There's an important distinction to be made between sponsorship and mentoring, so let's be clear.

A sponsor advocates for you when you're not in the room; he or she can make sure you gain the visibility and advocacy you need in an organization in order to be promoted.

A mentor, on the other hand, offers guidance and is usually outside the immediate sphere of influence in your organization. They are probably less directly influential with the people who decide your career, although they can be very helpful in offering informed advice and coaching. Indeed, mentors can benefit just as much from the experience as their mentees – the so-called 'reverse mentoring' effect. Heather Melville, Director of Client Experience at PwC and Chair of CMI Women, is a prominent champion of this.

The distinction is important because sponsorship is regarded as a more effective talent management strategy than straightforward mentoring. As one woman in a senior leadership role summed it up, 'The reason I got promoted each time was male sponsorship. I had three men in different parts of the business advocating for me and a line manager who asked them to support my case for promotion.[10]

3. Flexible and part-time working stigma: 'the parent (motherhood) trap'

> *'That whole, "so you can have it all." Nope. Not at the same time. That's a lie. And it's not always enough to lean in, because that sh*t doesn't work all the time.'*
> – Michelle Obama

Family caring responsibilities are still overwhelmingly the role of women. Despite being in existence for many years, take-up of paternity leave is still only 2 per cent in the UK. Far more women are working in part-time jobs, job shares, or taking extended career breaks when they have children than men.

And it's the issues those women face when returning from maternity leave or a childcare break that contribute to women's lack of advancement, as well as their poorer pay. The name for this is 'the motherhood penalty' and it has been studied widely across the world.

The motherhood penalty assumes that women with children simply cannot handle the same workload as their male counterparts. A recent study by the IFS found that mothers are earning about 30 per cent less than fathers by the time their first child has grown. A big driver for this is the lack of promotion and wage progression for part-time workers. The IFS reckons this explains about half of the gender pay gap, and is especially pronounced for well-educated women with graduate degrees.[11]

Women know that having children often leads to career setbacks. A survey by the Mumsnet website found that 91 per cent of mothers believe the motherhood penalty exists, with almost two-thirds (65 per cent) saying that having children had negatively impacted their career. The biggest negative impact for 56 per cent of women came from women feeling unable to pursue a promotion or commit to long hours because of family commitments – although, ironically, just over half of women felt they worked more efficiently since having children.[12] Changing perceptions about this is hard, as many companies will look at the issue through the wrong lens. As Mark Read, CEO of WPP told a group of women in communications, 'When we introduced more flexible working in the US the problem was the finance department said, "You can't do this, that policy is going to cost $1.2m, and two weeks' paternity leave is going to cost $1.5m." People can measure the cost of all these policies but what they can't measure is the cost of not having the policy. What about the five really talented women that leave and you have to re-recruit them and pay headhunters and all the costs . . . all of the things you can't measure in a business?'

Not only do women receive less pay, but men actually increase their earnings when fatherhood happens. One researcher found that while mothers earned on average 4 per cent less per child, fathers' pay actually increased by 6 per cent per child. Thus, the notion of the 'fatherhood bonus' was born. Fatherhood is perceived as a 'valued characteristic, signalling greater work commitment and stability', while mothers are viewed as 'exhausted and distracted'.[13]

In CMI's 'Blueprint for Balance', as well as in the Mumsnet survey, flexible working was also cited as an important way to help women in the workplace. But we found that the policy and practice of flexible working can often be at odds, and it can often backfire for women.

Firstly, it can lead to longer working hours overall. Those given the right to work flexibly often feel an increased motivation and commitment to 'give back' the gift of flexibility to their employers. Secondly, you simply work longer – even if you're not being paid as a result. And lastly, technology enables you to be always on – so you are working every time, everywhere.[14] As one woman said, 'I'm at 80% now, but I don't just work four days a week.'[15]

Then there's flexibility 'stigma'. In too many workplaces 'first in, last out' is still mistaken for productivity and commitment. I had my own epiphany here as a single mum going through a divorce. I was a global executive with a heavy travel schedule. I had been getting up at 4.30 a.m., flying to a European capital and flying back to put my child to bed at 8 p.m. But my new boss banned that, saying I had to stay on the road and take my European work colleagues out for dinner. It was what they expected from their senior leaders. After a few trial runs of excusing myself between courses to read my seven-year-old

Table 6: Perceived Problems of Flexible Working
Source: CMI 'A Blueprint for Balance' report, January 2018, p. 21

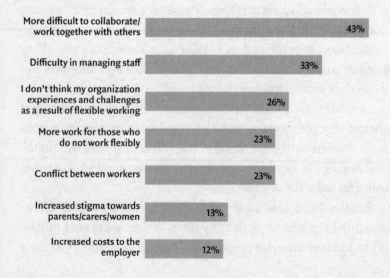

daughter *Anne of Green Gables* on the loo, I gave up and switched companies.

Men also face difficulties in admitting to childcare responsibilities. One woman told me the story of a male colleague lying about being stuck in traffic when he was really dropping his children at school. Another male CEO declined to share that he was attending a conference call from his daughter's sports day. Taking care of the children is still, it seems, perceived as emasculating. This serves only to reinforce gender stereotypes that men should not be sharing the responsibility of childcare.[16]

There are many pithy and poignant stories about flexible working. Here's one of my favourites.

A woman who works from home was surprised when her company arranged to visit her home office and decorate it in exactly the same style as her workplace. They explained that if the Americans or client teams saw her working from home she would be considered to be 'less significant' and not taken seriously.[17]

4. Recruitment, and talent and reward practices

In many organizations recruitment, training, progression and reward practices have gone wrong. This problem may be best described as 'fixing the women'. Most existing organizational processes have been designed by and for white men. I suggest that we need to adapt, modernize and change many of these if we expect them to work for women and other underrepresented groups.

Do we have the courage to change the legacy?

Recruitment

Having all-male shortlists is a bad idea, yet it still slips into play more often than it should – especially in sectors such as technology and engineering, and for positions such as CEOs, chairs and divisional presidents.

We need to stop defining requirements too conservatively, particularly for senior roles. If you're recruiting for a FTSE board chair, CEO or board committee chair, and you stipulate that the candidate must have prior experience in a similar role, then you'll get 90 per cent-plus applications from men. Search firms will, for their part, also reinforce those narrow requirements. As Moya Greene, former CEO of Canada's and the UK's Royal Mail said at the Hampton-Alexander Review launch in 2018, 'The requirements that we're setting that you must have been a CEO, or you must have been a CFO, are too rigid.'

Push back on your search firms, if you use them. I once had an HR director lament that he'd been through two search firms for technical executive positions and both had come up with all-male shortlists. I reckoned they weren't trying hard enough, as they were relying too heavily on a narrow set of experience criteria. To prove my point, I reached out to my network and within twenty-four hours had found a credible female candidate. PwC's Andy Woodfield puts it very well: 'It's only difficult to find people if you don't look. If you look in the mirror then you probably won't find anyone.'

Be aware of the language and job descriptions you're using in your ads. If you ask for 'strong', 'confident', 'competitive', 'driven' leaders, you're much more likely to end up with male applicants. An analysis by leading job sites in the USA and UK found that by changing the language to more gender-neutral descriptors, ads got a 40 per cent broader pool of applicants.

One leading UK job site analysed the most commonly used male- and female-gendered words in more than 75,000 job ads. Words such as 'lead', 'analyse', 'competitive', 'confident' were male; whereas 'support', 'responsible', 'understanding', 'committed' were female. They produced a 'gender bias decoder' you can use to check your job ads – and there are other apps as well.[18] The LinkedIn website enables recruiters to see how men and women respond differently to emails so that they can adjust their language and imagery.

And then there's 'blind recruitment'. In Iris Bohnet's book *What Works*, she tells a wonderful story of how the Boston Symphony Orchestra increased its number of female performers simply by introducing a curtain to prevent the assessment panel from seeing who was playing. They focused instead on the music, and the proportion of women in the orchestra rose from 5.5 per cent to 35 per cent.[19] More and more firms are promoting gender, social and ethnic diversity through blind CV recruitment.

Once you've got a gender-balanced pool of applicants, don't fall into the trap of having non-gender-balanced recruitment panels. If there is one woman on a shortlist and males are interviewing, the likely outcome is she won't get the job. And if you don't have a woman to sit on your panel, recruit one.

Talent management

Women can routinely be subjected to gender bias in performance reviews. A recent study showed that women are 1.4 times more likely to receive critical feedback based on gender and subjective judgements. Feedback for a woman might run along the lines of 'Heidi seems to shrink when she's around others . . . she needs to be more self-confident'; whereas the same problem of confidence might be given a positive spin when the recipient is male – 'Jim needs to develop his natural ability to work with people'.[20] More frequent feedback from a broader collection of reviewers can help overcome this, as can providing specific examples of what the person needs to do differently and better.

The language used to describe women versus men in performance reviews is reminiscent of McKinsey's 'micro-aggressions'. Women are much more likely to have their leadership styles described in negative terms as 'abrasive', 'bossy' or 'aggressive'. Such words were not found to be used in male performance reviews and, in the rare instances 'aggressive' is deployed, it's usually to encourage men to be *more* aggressive. As performance reviews often determine promotion, progression and pay, it's little wonder that women are held back.

Outmoded attitudes towards taking time out from work also disadvantage women when it comes to progression. Women's time off work is often viewed as having no value, and too many firms still promote people on the basis of time served rather than results.

Sometimes organizations train women to fit into and flourish within the existing culture and environment. When 'fixing the women' becomes the primary method of addressing gender bias, it only delivers superficial progress. This is the main criticism levelled at Facebook COO Sheryl Sandberg's *Lean In*.

In her book, Sandberg eloquently argues that women need to negotiate more, ask for promotions more and put themselves forward in order to boost their chances of advancement. But if that's all they do, it won't be enough. In fact, a subsequent study has found that those who subscribe solely to the 'lean in messages' are more likely to believe that women are responsible for causing and fixing the problems of gender balance.[21]

Unless and until broader processes are fixed as well, there

will be little advancement. As Melanie Richards, Deputy Chair of KPMG says, 'I always get a sense that people sometimes turn to fixing the women, and how do we make the women work and operate in the environments they're in? But encouraging inclusivity should surely be about changing the environment, not the women. "You can only lean in so far," says Cherie Blair, "if no one is there leaning out to catch you." '

A woman in a global technology company once told me how tired she was of the training to help female managers get noticed. She described the advice proffered that they should go into the bathroom before important meetings, look into the mirror and shout at themselves about how fabulous they were. Rather than appreciating women's distinctive leadership styles, she felt this programme was aimed at turning them into 'alpha males'.

Unfortunately, a lot of diversity training doesn't work. A study by *Harvard Business Review* found a number of flaws, particularly if such training is mandatory, aimed at senior managers, and only talks about the importance of avoiding lawsuits. In fact, this kind of approach can make matters worse by exposing people (often men) to others' biases and normalizing them. Far from solving the issue, the firms examined for this study actually went backwards in terms of their diversity.[22]

Women's networks

Women's networks are often used to promote women. I belong to several. But there's one very important thing to remember: there are only women present at women-only events. And given most senior positions are held by men, it is absolutely essential that you network and engage with men as well as women. This is how you'll change the status quo and improve your own and other women's chances of progression. This is why many women's networks are trying to include men. We have a man on the board of CMI Women and always aim to include men in events. I recently attended a Women in Finance event at which about one-third of the participants were men. As the founder of one women's network says, 'Our members see that as long as men are in charge, if we don't bring them along [and] if they don't bring us along . . . nothing will change.'[23]

Fixing the broader processes, rather than just fixing women, is vital to success.

5. The confidence gap

> 'Men overtrade the whole time, they blag their way in through the front door. Women don't express the same level of confidence. They sit there and wait for somebody else to tell them they're ready.'
> – Bruce Carnegie-Brown, President of CMI and Chairman of Lloyd's of London

Having just told you that leaning in doesn't work on its own, I am now going to admit that women DO need to up their confidence in order to improve gender balance at work.

Consider this widely told anecdote: if a woman sees ten attributes listed for a job and she is sure she meets nine, she will stress about the one that she doesn't meet. If a man meets six out of ten characteristics, he'll conclude that he's clearly the best candidate and can learn the others on the job. Says Moya Greene, former Royal Mail CEO, 'We have had sometimes to put our hands in the small of people's backs – very, very capable women – and say, "You go for this." Women, for some reason, think they have to have every single one of the traits down 100 per cent. And of course there are no perfect candidates for anything.'

The same holds true for salary and bonus negotiations. In a speech one Chair said: 'I have never, ever had a woman ask for a pay rise. There isn't a list long enough for all the men who've asked.'[24] Some progressive employers are dealing with this by not asking for prior salaries and making salaries non-negotiable. Some US states are passing laws to prevent employers from asking about salary history.

Lack of confidence frequently spills over into harmful behaviours at work. If a woman has to leave early to pick up her kids, she'll often excuse herself by saying, 'Sorry, so sorry, I've got to leave the meeting early to go pick up the kids because the nanny's got flu and I've got to get them to music lessons, really sorry to go.' A man will stand up and leave with a simple 'got to go now'. No explanation, no apology. I've witnessed it many times.

Many accomplished women are still subject to self-doubt. Sheryl Sandberg devotes a whole chapter in *Lean In* to 'imposter syndrome' – the feeling that one's success and accomplishments are somehow not deserved and the fear that one day they will be exposed as a fraud. In their book *The Confidence Code*, Katty Kay and Claire Shipman say they've encountered it even among super-successful women such as Hillary Clinton and Christine Lagarde.

Women, they say, have a tendency to overthink things, coupled with a drive for perfectionism. This often results in higher stress levels for women and girls who are struggling to have it all.

Confidence is the stuff that turns thoughts into action, say Kay and Shipman. Women often can't do this because they are too inside their own heads.

I have witnessed this in some of the brightest scientific minds in Britain, through my involvement with Women of Influence, a mentoring programme set up by Cancer Research UK to help develop their female fellows. A group of successful business women from many sectors helped raise money for the fellows and then mentored them. These women were among the top scientists in the world. Yet when mentoring them I found that many doubted their own abilities to do things such as apply for promotion. The answer was to ask them to keep an achievement log as if they were one of their male colleagues. Doing this, they quickly overcame their reticence and listed their accomplishments. Then when I asked them to objectively benchmark their achievements versus colleagues', they could put themselves in the top 10 per cent.

Why are women less confident than men? There are many reasons and I don't have space to go into them here. Some are biological – such as the absence of testosterone – and some are learned behaviours.

In her book *A Good Time to be a Girl*, Dame Helena Morrissey discusses a number of differences between men and women. Men are more inclined towards systems and women towards empathy, she argues. Men and women are different in leadership as well, she says, with men being more confident, decisive and risk-taking in their decisions; women are more thoughtful, collaborative and participatory.

Ultimately, I believe it's much better to have a balance – neither all male characteristics nor all female. I agree with Helena's phrase: 'Don't lean in, change the system.' She concludes, 'This is not about adopting the trappings of male power, but about redefining power, *changing rather than mimicking* the power structures that [women] have been largely excluded from in the past.'[25]

A lack of self-confidence has a lot to do with how girls are raised. Many young girls I speak to are still afraid to fail. One school I know ran a failure clinic to try to teach them this. The boys seem to learn it more readily.

Sometimes teachers are the perpetrators. And sometimes we mindlessly reinforce gender stereotypes. My female director with young children was appalled to hear a primary school Mother's Day song: 'My mummy may not have a degree, but she cooks and cleans and serves my tea.' Speaking at the Hampton-Alexander Review, Miriam González Durántez, a founder of Speakers for Schools, explained how she regularly comes across the assumption from children that male speakers are a doctor, banker or boss. If the speaker is a woman, children assume she's a teacher, nurse or mother.

Opt-out syndrome

Faced with a mountain of cultural and practical obstacles, many women decide to opt out. 'I know many of my peer group of capable women who decided that going for senior roles is not what they wanted,' says Carolyn Fairbairn, Director-General of the CBI.

I've first-hand experience of 'opt-out syndrome' after three roles as the first and only woman at C-suite level. I decided to move from the UK to the USA, took a career sabbatical, focused on caring for my family, and came back four years later into the not-for-profit sector. It is still much more acceptable for women to do this than men. Other women who opt out start their own small businesses. It's particularly common in sectors where few women reach the top and where, therefore, there are few role models.

Barclays' research found that 69 per cent of senior women wanted to start their own business compared with only 29 per cent of men. Even the entrepreneurs face enormous hurdles. Sadly, only 2.2 per cent of the $85bn in venture capital in the USA went to female-founded start-ups in 2018.[26]

Many talented women who are about to break through into C-suite roles, but instead strike out on their own, tell me they no longer want to fight to fix the system. What a loss!

In summary

After every talk I give on gender balance (and I give a lot), I am approached by women confirming the findings in this chapter. They share anecdotes and stories of how they have been treated badly at work and the obstacles that get in their way.

Still, sometimes you just have to laugh. Sarah Cooper is an ex-Google employee turned stand-up comic who recently

| Figure 11: Finding a Mistake

Pointing out a mistake is always risky so it's important to always apologize for noticing the mistake and then make sure that no one thinks you're too sure about it. People will appreciate your 'Hey what do I know?!' sensibilities

released a book called *How to be Successful without Hurting Men's Feelings: Non-threatening Leadership Strategies for Women.* She has a witty take on how to approach a familiar working situation.[27] (See Figure 11 opposite.)

What Other Experts Say

What are the main pitfalls to progress in achieving gender balance?

Paul Polman (former CEO, Unilever; Impact Champion, HeforShe)

'. . . there is a fatigue creeping in and we need to change the narrative . . . I think there are the usual barriers . . . resistance because "she may take my job" type thing, or lack of understanding, a lack of resources to attack it, or a belief that others do it, or a lack of data – all that stuff exists to some extent. So you have to work it on multiple fronts.'

Carolyn Fairbairn (Director-General, CBI)

'It can be easy to fall into the trap of thinking there must be one silver bullet, but it's a whole system change. We need more of our CEOs to put gender equality to the top of the list.'

Julia Gillard (former Australian Prime Minister; Chair, Global Institute for Women's Leadership, King's College, London)

'Number one, taking it seriously, actually thinking about the strategies for change. Number two, calling out sexism when it's apparent . . . And we still know that much of how people see woman leaders is gendered and so we do need to call out the gender bit when we see that applied to women politicians. And then thirdly, I think for occupations, you know, whether it's politics, whether it's occupations like politics that are full of intensity, full of travel, there's still work to do to help people balance work and family life.'

Brenda Trenowden (Global Chair, 30% Club)

'Gender stereotypes, norms and biases are really one of the biggest barriers. We're still very much in a society [that has] had strong masculine stereotypes in terms of who we think leaders are and who we think should be running companies . . . I think culture is the other big issue. A lot of industries and big companies have difficulty retaining and sometimes at- tracting women because there is one dominant type of cul- ture, and women decide that they're not going to stick it out because it's not inclusive and it doesn't allow them to really thrive.'

Heather Melville OBE (Chair, CMI Women; Director of Client Experience, PwC)

'If I can speak really honestly, I think women themselves [are a barrier] because sometimes we doubt our own ability and we need to get more women feeling confident within themselves – myself included.'

Melanie Richards (Deputy Chair, KPMG UK)

'I actually think the biggest barrier is being much more mind- ful about the willingness to include everybody in a conversa- tion. And what I always say is actually if you're getting this right for women, you're probably getting it right for the quiet man in your organization . . . who is never going to get heard while you structure your organization around a particular stereotype of what you think good leadership looks like.'

Sam Smethers (CEO, Fawcett Society)

'I don't think there is as yet a really creative and sophisticated understanding about how you could structure work differently, particularly in the top of organizations. I think we're very slow to design work differently.'

Sarah Gordon (former Business Editor, *Financial Times*)

'The key obstacle is sexism, don't you think? . . . I see a lot of chief executives who think that they are on the right page about this. It's not just about increasing gender balance but, in general, more general measures of diversity . . . they are unaware of their own deep-seated attitudes and they don't do as much as is necessary . . . It's not enough to have a flexible working policy. You have to really appreciate it's really hard work.'

Dame Cilla Snowball (former group Chairman and group CEO, AMV BBDO; Chair, Women's Business Council, UK)

'I think the pitfalls are thinking that one woman on a board will solve the problem. That one woman in the exec-team or a promotion solves the problem.'

4 Five Practices That Work for Organizations

| Figure 12: 5 Practices That Work for Organizations

 To address your gender pay gap, set a target, tie performance evaluations to achieving it, measure your progress against it, and regularly monitor and report on that progress

 Put in place a well-run and structured sponsorship programme for women. Sponsors truly believe in the talent of their 'sponsees' and are much more likely to advocate for them when they are not in the room

5 Practices That Work for Organizations

Change your recruitment and progression practices to make them more gender aware. Set 50/50 promotion targets for men and women and adopt diversity practices for recruitment

Use men as change agents to challenge stereotypes and set an example that it's okay to champion women. 75% of men feel they should contribute to gender initiatives

 Embrace flexible working. Measure outputs, not face time; train line managers; avoid a 'one-size-fits-all' approach; and role-model and support from the top

Now we come to the solutions. We are seeing examples of progress, and we can accelerate it by being relentless in the pursuit of the practical, the positive and those initiatives that deliver measurable impact.

Looking across the landscape of informed opinion, I suggest that these are the top five practices to champion and adopt if you want your organization to make progress.

1 Transparency, targets and monitoring
2 Gender-aware recruitment and promotion policies
3 Flexible working that works for all
4 An inclusive culture at every level that also engages men
5 Sponsorship and mentoring programmes

1. Transparency, targets and monitoring

Transparency and targets come in two types. First, there are macro-level initiatives that involve collaboration between government, business groups, the media and other stakeholders. These initiatives tend to look at transparency, targets and quotas, as well as aggregated monitoring.

Then there are firm-level targets sponsored by leaders. All these are, of course, interlinked. Most effect is achieved when efforts and impacts are combined.

Quotas
Perhaps the most common macro-level intervention is to set quotas for women on boards. This has happened in much of Western Europe. Eight of the top twelve countries with the highest percentages of women on boards have achieved this via quotas. California, home to some of the world's largest

companies and the fifth-largest world economy by GDP, has adopted a quota policy requiring one woman on all public company boards by the end of 2019; and up to three by 2021.

There is little doubt that quotas drive change. The countries that operate them have seen most progress in the number of women on boards. The risk, of course, is that these changes are forced and superficial, rather than owned and embedded in the values of an organization. Nonetheless, the increase in numbers of women on boards has undoubtedly been driven in large part by quotas. However, quotas are a peripheral point here, as most readers won't be in a position to enact them. Indeed, many businesses oppose them. I sympathize, as I believe that most organizations want to – and should – own their business agendas. Greater diversity is, as we have seen in Chapter 1, a healthy business driver that should be pursued in its own right. I am delighted that there seems to be another way to achieve progress. Results in Australia, Canada and the UK, based on voluntary transparency and targets and joint government and private efforts, are proof of this.

CASE STUDY

Women on boards: the UK story

In February 2011, Mervyn Davies announced the recommendations of his 'Women on Boards' review. These said that the number of women on FTSE 100 boards should increase from 12.55 per cent to 25 per cent by 2015; the number hit 26 per cent in 2015. When Davies launched there were 52 all-male boards in the FTSE 100.

The Davies Review worked very closely with the Government Equalities Office (then the Department of Business, Industry and

Skills) and the 30% Club. The latter draws its name from its signature approach of setting a target regarded as a 'tipping point' for gender balance – 30% – and enrolling the chairs and chief executives of the FTSE 350 to join the 'club' of enlightened men to advocate for change. Importantly, the 2015 report stated that progress – which needed to be evidenced – should be achieved voluntarily, without quotas.

In 2015, the Hampton-Alexander Review (named after the business leaders Sir Philip Hampton and the late Dame Helen Alexander) took over where Davies left off. It was decided to set further targets for the thorny issue of FTSE 350 executive committees and those who report directly into them.

In September 2018 the percentage of women on FTSE 100 boards hit 30 per cent and there were no more all-male boards. The Hampton-Alexander Review has set a target of 33 per cent representation of women on FTSE 350 boards and is using the same mechanisms as the Davies Review to fix the pipeline of upcoming talent. As of November 2018 the progress since the start of the Davies Review in 2011 was not insignificant – although the pace is lacking, especially in the 250. In a year:

Executive committees and direct reports increased from 25.2 per cent to 27 per cent.
FTSE 250 increased from 24 per cent to 24.9 per cent.
FTSE 100 boards increased from 27 per cent to 30.2 per cent.
FTSE 250 boards increased from 22.8 per cent to 24.9 per cent.

Aligned pressure across stakeholders

The 30% Club and Hampton-Alexander Review (and the Davies Review before it) are clear that multiple stakeholders must work together to achieve results on gender balance. This includes media, investors, headhunters and other stakeholders. As a chair put it: '[It's about applying] peer pressure, media pressure, shareholder pressure, government pressure and, I think it's fair to say, encouraging women's aspirations as well.'

The UK media – and UK-based global media – play an important role in keeping gender progress at the top of the agenda. It's particularly important that they give top-quality editorial news or business space to the issue, rather than treating it as a women's or lifestyle issue. The *Financial Times*, *Times* and *Sunday Times*, BBC and *Guardian* are particularly good in this respect. Alison Brittain, CEO of Whitbread, made the important observation that, 'There's nothing large companies like less than being featured negatively in the press.'

Equally important is the pressure exerted by investors, who have identified gender as a key stewardship issue. Deborah Gilshan co-chairs the 30% Club's investor group, a global coalition of more than 33 investors with $11trn of assets under management, and which includes giants such as Blackrock. Gilshan says that performance on gender issues has become a real matter of reputation, and that investors are asking chairs and CEOs as a matter of course about their gender reporting progress.

The Investment Association (IA) in the UK is upping the importance it attaches to gender balance; so far four out of ten of their members have made voting decisions based on gender diversity. 'Firms who have been slow to act are now finding themselves well and truly under the spotlight,' says Andrew Ninian, the IA's director of stewardship and corporate governance, 'as asset managers increasingly take into account gender representation when voting at AGMs.'[1]

Such voluntary pressures from the media, peers and investors may be enough for big companies, and the public sector, but in most countries small businesses constitute the overwhelming number of employers – in the UK, for example, small and medium-sized enterprises (SMEs) are 99 per cent of all businesses. So we must continue to enrol stakeholder groups and extend the transparency of reporting to include every business. In this manner, pressure from employees will grow over time.

Voluntary 'coalition of the willing' efforts work for the following reasons.

- They are out to prove that progress can be made without quotas.
- They are supported by chairs and CEOs of a well-defined group of companies (for example, all FTSE 350 firms).
- They have clear, ambitious targets, very transparent and increasingly comprehensive reporting, and regular progress measurement spotlighted by the media.
- They include other stakeholders, most notably investors, regulators, search firms, professional services firms and other business groups.
- They foster a sense of competition and the collegiate – no one wants to be left out.
- They 'fame and name' the leaders and 'name and shame' the laggards.

The more we use these mechanisms, the more likely success will come sooner. Australia's swift progress with women on boards backs this up. The 30% Club is already global – there are ten chapters, with more on the way.

Coalitions of the willing work.

CEO-led targets for the organization

> 'I'm a simple guy, if you want to improve something
> you've got to measure it. And you've got to be transparent
> about it. And you know there are going to be some good
> things and some things to improve on.'
> – Jan Zijderveld, CEO, Avon Products[2]

I know of no company, large or small, that has made significant progress on this agenda without a clear target that is cascaded down throughout the line. This transparency needs to be carried out in every quartile, and targets embedded at every organizational level.

The work on targets needs to be led by the CEO and leadership team. And progress against the targets must be measured. As Philip Hampton, Chair of the Hampton-Alexander Review, has said, 'In terms of what works when improving gender diversity, you first and foremost need strong leadership. If the company, board and top management believe that gender diversity is important then it will almost certainly be addressed.'[3]

Paul Polman's story

Paul Polman, CEO of Unilever from 2009 to 2019, was one of the first CEOs to champion gender balance. He did this long before it was fashionable. He topped the *FT*'s 'HERoes' list in 2018 and was a founder of the UN initiative HeforShe.

Paul built Unilever's gender diversity from 37 per cent to 48 per cent globally and to 50 per cent on the board.

This includes challenging countries such as Saudi Arabia
and India and functions such as factory work and sales.
The office environment has an even higher percentage of
women, as borne out by the UK's gender pay gap figures:
2.5 per cent in favour of women in the UK overall
and 3 per cent in global functional roles based at the
London HQ. He explains, 'I've always taken a broader
approach . . . I've taken a tack of a total gender balance
of posts across our total value chain. So if we retrain
smallholder farmers we want 50 per cent to be women.
[When] we work with retailers we want 50 per cent to
be women. Small businesses that we support financially
50 per cent women . . . so in everything that we do we
apply a gender lens . . . And it creates a very strong
commitment because the influence we can have across
our value chain is even significantly higher than the
influence we can have by looking only at our own shop.'

Polman puts his progress down to leadership and
culture. 'Do you really want it? Is the CEO committed?
Do you get the tone on the top? You need to get the
right culture. Otherwise you force it in and you get a
revolving door. You might get more people in because
you are committed, but if the organization has the wrong
culture, which you see in many places, you'll get the
leaky bucket anyway.'

He admits he had to work very hard to get there
because of basic gender bias and a culture where
men were still dominant. 'You have to be incredibly
thorough and disciplined about your merit system and
to counter all these perceived arguments like, "Ah, now
he's promoting women but they don't really deserve it or
they haven't shown the leadership; you know [it's only]

because he wants to achieve these numbers." ' Polman put rigorous merit systems and scorecards in place and combined them with targets, technology and tracking in hiring, promotion and other metrics – reviewed on a monthly basis. 'Treasure what you measure,' he sums up.

One thing Polman won't do is tie gender balance to pay. In his pre-Unilever days he got a bonus for championing diversity. He gave it back. 'I said, I don't want that bonus. I want you to go after the people that don't do it. You shouldn't reward what we should all be doing. You should correct the behaviour of people that is dysfunctional, otherwise you can never get it into the culture.' He compares it with factory safety. 'We don't reward a factory manager if the factory is safe but we certainly fire a factory manager if we have safety issues.'

An ardent feminist, Polman thinks the qualities of purpose, long-term focus, collaboration and authenticity are more present in women than men. His advice to women reflects this: 'Be yourself. Don't change. We need your style. We need you as a human being the way you are.'

His second ask of women is to help other women, through networks, encouragement and what he calls 'holding the door open'.

And for men? Apart from standing up for women, and signing up for HeforShe, 'Men need to understand and be able to explain that it's not a zero-sum game; that we all win when women are supported. It's as good for men as it is for women.' His advice for the laggards is stark. '[For companies], it's a question of either changing or perishing. It's that simple.'

Almost every success story involves setting targets at every level and then tracking them through. Virgin Money, for example, faced a very large 36 per cent pay gap. The firm set a target to achieve 50/50 gender balance by 2020 and then created an app that allows every manager to instantly see the impact of a certain pay rise or promotion decision on the gender pay gap in their area of the business.

Since 2016, Virgin Money has closed the gap by over 6 percentage points, to just under 30 per cent. And this is financial services, one of the worst-performing of all sectors when it comes to gender balance. The company acknowledges that it still has a long way to go and that the key will be in getting more women into senior roles, thus addressing their 'glass pyramid'.

In another intractable sector, mining, BHP Billiton made a bold commitment to have 50 per cent of its Australian workforce female by 2025, up from 17 per cent. They targeted a 3 per cent increase per year in the percentage of women in their teams, and linked the performance and pay of managers to achieving this goal. The company has increased its female workforce by some 40 per cent since the initiative was announced and is on track to achieve its commitment in 2018.[4]

CASE STUDY

Salesforce

The software giant Salesforce chose to eradicate its own gender pay gap, spending $3m in 2015 to help achieve this. CEO Marc Benioff was concerned by instances when he found himself in all-male managerial meetings. In 2013, he began a programme called the 'Women's Surge' to bring about gender equality.

The company introduced a requirement that at least a third of participants at any meeting should be female.

The programme brought to light the state of unequal pay at Salesforce and, initially, Benioff struggled to believe it. But after commissioning a review of all the employees' salaries, it became clear that something had to be done. The decision was taken to raise all women's salaries to that of their male counterparts. Benioff's decision to champion pay equity has encouraged other companies to release their annual data on pay gaps.

CASE STUDY

Diageo

Diageo is widely recognized as a pioneer in diversity by design; the firm ranked eleventh globally for gender equality in a study conducted by Equileap. CEO Ivan Menezes received the Male Champion of Change award from the UK Women's Business Council in 2018. In his acceptance speech, Menezes attributed their success to 'the commitment at the highest levels to make change happen, and the action on the ground to make that vision a reality'. He acknowledged the strong business case for diversity and, on a personal level, shared that his primary motivator is 'creating an environment where every individual is trusted, valued and included'. Just eight years ago, the executive committee consisted entirely of men. Today, 40 per cent are women. The percentage of women in roles directly below board and executive level stands at 37 per cent, with the goal of achieving 40 per cent by 2025.

Diageo ensures 50 per cent of graduate recruits are female and that all roles have diverse slates. Menezes says it's equally important to invest in culture, 'creating an environment where women want to work and where they thrive'. Now that there are more women at the top of the organization, they are encouraged to get involved as role models as well. His view is that 'having women at the top of an organization creates a virtuous cycle of gender progression within and outside of business', but that 'it's just as important that men share this ambition for equality too'. Ivan reveals that the median pay gap across the UK has improved to 5.4 per cent, down from 8.6 per cent in 2017.

Greater diversity has improved the business, encouraging 'healthy tension, less group-think, better decision-making', says Menezes. And today, in the historically male-dominated whisky industry, 50 per cent of Diageo's expert Johnnie Walker blending team are women.

CASE STUDY

Lululemon

In 2017, Celeste Burgoyne, Lululemon's Executive Vice-President for the Americas, made a commitment to achieving gender pay parity, spurred on by the revelation that at the current rate of change, the gender pay gap wouldn't be closed until 2059. On 8 March 2017, the luxury sportswear brand announced its intention to achieve equal pay for equal work by the end of 2018 for all 14,000 employees. Despite encountering substantial difficulties when their CEO had to step down, they remained committed to achieving pay parity at the company, where women make up 75 per cent of the overall workforce and comprise 90 per cent of the employees in their retail stores. This goal was realized six months earlier than planned. Collaboration with all employees ensured teams still had confidence in the business.[5]

I encourage you to set an ambitious target for gender balance and measure the progress you make towards it. Make it as important as any other business initiative. Even if you're not a large company, you can still use these techniques to make progress.

- Set a target.
- Tie performance evaluations and pay to achieving it.
- Measure your progress against it.
- Regularly monitor and report on that progress.

Progress can also be made at sector level. Take the Women in Finance Charter, a sector initiative sponsored by the UK's Treasury and championed by Dame Jayne-Anne Gadhia, formerly of Virgin Money. It calls for progression of women into senior roles, target-setting and public reporting on progress, alongside ensuring pay is linked to gender diversity targets.

In the USA, organizations such as Parity.org and the Women Tech Council have set up programmes to create and monitor opportunities for women.

Workfront

One small company in a challenged sector that championed diversity successfully is the start-up Workfront, based in Salt Lake City. Its President and

CEO Alex Shootman told me how proud he is to have a 50/50 leadership team in the tech sector. It's a great story.

In late 2017, the company launched an employee resource group called 'Women of Workfront', which creates a community for the female employees at the company, who participate together in community initiatives, educational opportunities and 'Lean In Circles'. In a company where women account for 50 per cent of executive leadership, all vice-presidents sign the 'Parity Pledge', a commitment that they will interview a female candidate for every role they have open on their teams.

It's working. Workfront has seen an increase in female hires, as well as a double-digit drop in attrition of women. As Laura Butler, Senior Vice-President of people and culture, points out, that retention figure is a massive win for the company. 'Filling the boat and having it leak at the same time isn't good.'

If you work in the UK, it is easy to benchmark your company because all organizations with more than 250 employees must report on the following:

- the mean salary of men versus women
- the median salary of men versus women
- bonuses and the percentage of men versus women who get them, and
- the percentage of men versus women in every quartile of the organization by pay band.

Of course, as KPMG's Melanie Richards puts it, 'It's not just about having abstract data, it's understanding what goes on below the surface, tracking how many people make their way through the organization, and doing diagnostics which include qualitative as well as quantitative analysis.' You need to understand the reasons behind your results when you analyse your own data and set your targets. What are your particular challenges? Have you spoken to people about your results?

So much of this is about leaders understanding the true human aspects of the issue.

2. Gender-aware recruitment and promotion policies

It all starts with how you recruit. Many companies are realizing that their recruitment ads contain innate gender bias that can put off women. Accenture made the language it used to recruit IT professionals more female-friendly, and saw a greater share of female applicants. The intriguing start-up Textio uses AI software to identify words that put women off. When the Australian software giant Atlassian used Textio's software, it saw an 80 per cent increase in the hiring of women in technical roles over a two-year period.[6]

Once you've got the language right, make sure you get a balanced list of candidates. Always aim for 50/50 wherever possible. Having only one woman on the list means she is unlikely to be appointed, according to research from the UK's behavioural science 'nudge' unit.

Expand what you consider your talent pool. Defining this too narrowly excludes, for example, women who may have a CV gap. Too many employers view this negatively. This is a shame, because time away from work can also increase life skills and flexibility. Increasingly, career gaps aren't just about raising kids anyway – many millennials take time out to go travelling.

Executive search firms must adopt more gender-aware practices. In the UK, search firms now have to report back into the Department for Business, Innovation and Skills (BIS) and the Government Equalities Office on the percentage of women candidates they put forward for executive positions as well as the number they actually place. This should create greater transparency about candidate lists for senior positions being filled externally – a key enabler of progress. As recently as December 2018, global search firm Egon Zehnder reported that 75 per cent of board positions were still going to men in the 141 countries they studied. Transparency around the number of women candidates who progress to interview stage should help improve this ratio. And make sure you use balanced hiring panels, comprising both men and women equally if possible.

Use structured interview questions that ask all candidates exactly the same questions. Iris Bohnet shows how evaluating answers by question, rather than by candidate, can go a long way towards improving outcomes for women, as can asking candidates to perform the skills they will actually need while on the job. At a minimum, by asking all candidates the same questions and having a structured scoring sheet for the answers, you are forcing interviewers to rely on evidence from the candidates that they meet the requirements rather than a 'good vibe' or feeling, or a connection because of a shared acquaintance or background.[7]

The Women's Business Council, along with CMI's 'Blueprint for Balance', offers free toolkits to help achieve this.[8]

Targets

Women get promoted less frequently than men. This drives the 'glass pyramid' phenomenon whereby the majority of junior roles are filled by women but, as the roles become more senior, men dominate.

It follows, then, that you cannot fix your gender pay gap without fixing the promotion gap and ensuring you promote men and women at least equally. This applies not only to internal promotions but, crucially, also to externally recruited senior roles. The UK government agrees.

So what are the best ways of evening out promotion opportunities?

For starters, use a transparent, structured and monitored process for promotions. Why not set a 50/50 promotion ratio as a simple target for all line managers in your organization? The media company Sky did this, and with very impressive results. Similarly, it tasked every senior manager with promoting one or two more women than last year and saw an increased promotion rate for women. The same effect happened when Sky started reviewing women first – including those who had just returned from maternity leave – before progressing on to the men.

Pay and bonus transparency and monitoring

Most women think that they are likely to be paid less than experienced male hires, and the facts suggest they are correct. So how do you mitigate this?

Pay and bonus transparency are great places to start. Extending transparency to the decisions that underpin pay and bonuses can help close pay gaps – though it can be controversial.

The reality is that women just don't negotiate over pay as much; and bonuses tend to favour men. You can mitigate this by introducing pay bands, making people aware of them, and encouraging women to negotiate. Measuring bonuses paid to women and men, and setting a check-and-balance committee of senior leaders to review these, can also offset discrepancies.

Disclosing pay is, of course, still sensitive territory. But publishing pay bands for each level, as well as sharing and reviewing bonus structures for all employees, and benchmarking by gender, can make a vital contribution towards pay equality.[9] LinkedIn recently adopted a new practice that is working. As Joshua Graff, UK Country Manager and VP, LinkedIn Marketing Solutions, EMEA and LATAM, recently explained, 'We started a gender pay aware recruitment process whereby we narrowed the salary bands at which somebody could come in so there was ... almost no room for negotiation, so that certainly helped the situation. Internally, every individual also has the ability to see the band in which they sit ... they have full transparency and that's relatively new for us. We rolled it out over the last six months and it's working well.'

Returners programmes

A visible 'returners programme' can work wonders and boost promotion rates for women. Women who take career breaks frequently fall behind their peers when being considered for promotions. Part of this relates to line manager prejudice regarding time spent not working, but it's also partly down to lack of a transparent and formalized process for encouraging this talent pool to return to work.

As Carolyn Fairbairn, Director-General of the CBI, says, 'There continues to be the question of how can we better engage women returning from maternity leave? It is a question that business still does not yet have a solution to, even though progress is being made. There is often a sense of lost confidence coming back into the workplace and we need to find a more effective way to engage women returning to the workforce.'

Firms must stay in close touch with such women, says Fairbairn, and have a proper returners programme that doesn't assume that returning women want an easier staff job and, therefore, a less profitable career track.

Over a third of the companies in the Bloomberg GEI have structured returners programmes. According to PwC, returners programmes either exist or are being created in just over half of the companies they surveyed. PwC's report also found that although 76 per cent of professional women want to return to work, three in five highly skilled women ended up in lower-skilled and lower-paid jobs.[10]

So what do such successful returners programmes look like? Here are some important things to consider when setting one up.

1 **Decide what type of programme you want** – and ensure you have buy-in and a business case. Programmes can be supported internship programmes that run for three months and lead to a permanent hire if successful, or supported onboarding programmes that lead to permanent roles.

2 **Make sure your programme builds in flexible working**. Decide in advance the range of options you will allow, including where people work, when they work and how much they work. Can they work from home as well as the office? Can they work core hours – i.e. avoiding

meetings at school drop-off times – and also after hours if need be, for example, after children are in bed? Will you allow job shares, part-time working and shortened weeks? Will you allow more time off if people need that for caring responsibilities or childcare issues? The more flexible you can be in adapting this to each individual's circumstances, the more successful your programme will be. Try to avoid one-size-fits-all.

3 **Is your programme supported?** Do the CEO and senior management support the programme as a mainstream talent source? Are line managers trained on how to manage the programme participants well and fairly? Do you provide additional support for returners, such as induction training, coaching, mentoring and workplace buddies?

4 **Are you recruiting in the right places and in the right way?** Do you target places and resources where returners are likely to be found, such as web communities, specialist recruitment agencies and networking groups? Do you advertise your positions as flexible? Do you actively encourage returner applicants?[11]

CASE STUDY

How to create a successful returners programme

Hit Return

A collaboration between Mars, Vodafone and Centrica in the UK, Hit Return provides experienced professionals with a twelve-week paid internship programme, including practical work and coaching, to help them bridge successfully back into the workplace. This programme recognizes that people who return to work often have practical experiences – both in and out of work – that are undervalued. By giving returners a role in your organization, and combining this with flexible and tailored working opportunities, you can attract world-class talent to your organization and create a competitive advantage.

UBS Career Comeback Programme

Investment bank UBS has a unique career comeback programme aimed at people who have taken a career break of a minimum of two years. 'We're aiming for director and senior-level roles and we've found a huge wealth of talent that were operating at that level before taking a break, but who are being overlooked by standard recruiting methods,' says Carolanne Minashi, Global Head of Diversity and Inclusion at UBS.

'As all organizations struggle to find women to fill senior leadership roles, we think we have access to a new talent pool that, with a bit of creative support, can make a fabulous contribution to the business.' Retention is currently 100 per cent after a one-year pilot.

The programme has two offerings: a conventional twenty-week internship-style programme in New York; and a permanent-hire programme running in Zurich and London. Minashi understands the financial impact for women returners. Many organizations discount pay on these programmes, and it can be hard to bring salary levels back in line. 'We're not entertaining the idea of discounting pay. If people are coming at senior levels, we are paying them at senior levels.'

Restarting a career after a break period is not straightforward. The process has challenged UBS's standard recruitment practices. 'Algorithms don't work in this case,' says Minashi.

Line managers and recruiters need training and support to help them look past the break and at the skills, competencies and life experience the candidate brings.

There are many sources of information about returners programmes. A number of agencies, such as Return Hub, specialize in placing returners. Other organizations and businesses, such as My Family Care in the UK and Path Forward in the USA, help companies design returners programmes and signpost these for potential applicants. (The Path Forward website lists 70-plus programmes; Runneth London lists more than 30.)

Changing your recruitment and progression practices to make them more gender-aware really DOES make a difference. According to a global report from PwC, 71 per cent of organizations that adopted diversity practices reported a positive impact on their recruitment of female talent; 39 per cent increased the number of female applicants.

3. Flexible working that works for all

Flexible – also called agile or dynamic – working is creating exciting opportunities for the whole workforce, and especially women. According to research from UK charity Timewise, 87 per cent of the overall workforce wants to work flexibly.

The appeal cuts across all demographics: 84 per cent of men and 91 per cent of women would prefer to work flexibly; 92 per cent of people in the 18 to 34 bracket say they'd like to work flexibly. Indeed, 63 per cent of full-time workers already work flexibly in some way. Flexible working is on its way to becoming a social norm.

There's a ton of evidence that stacks up in support of the case for flexible working. The Task Force on Flexible Working, a UK government-sponsored initiative of which CMI is a member, chaired by CIPD (the professional body for HR), pulled together a comprehensive and highly convincing business case for flexible working that goes well beyond gender diversity. Specifically, it found that flexible working:

- encouraged employees to 'go the extra mile' for their employers
- had higher levels of job satisfaction and employee engagement that could result in as much as a 20 per cent performance improvement
- boosted motivation: nine out of ten employees felt it was a more important motivator than financial incentives; and 81 per cent felt it made them more productive
- reduced absence rates and stress, and increased well-being, especially among those with caring responsibilities, as well as increased workforce diversity by attracting parents and lower-income households
- helped retain staff at all levels, including senior levels, and reduced staff turnover by as much as 87 per cent, and
- helped organizations be more responsive to customer demand and more agile and competitive.[12]

So how can organizations implement flexible working successfully? Here are my top techniques, again drawing on the findings from the Task Force on Flexible Working.

Specify flexible working in recruitment ads

Right now, only 11 per cent of roles are currently advertised as flexible. That's a huge mismatch with the 87 per cent of people who want to work flexibly. When you advertise roles as flexible, you can attract top talent that might otherwise be out of reach. I recruited CMI's CFO that way; it was a key reason she joined us. Ask senior women candidates what arrangements they previously enjoyed, and offer to match them. Virgin Money has done this, with great results.

Design jobs to fit people

Avoid a 'one size fits all' approach to flexible working. If you have a top candidate, flex the time/role requirements to their needs. Similarly, avoid defining flexible working in a broadbrush way. Allow each employee to define their own menu of how they wish to work flexibly, rather than offering all employees the same approach.

Measure outputs, not face time

This is crucial. It's the main stigma many flexible workers face. Avoid creating a 'long hours' workplace culture where those first in and last out are assumed to be the most productive. Rather, make sure that each employee has clear objectives and measure their performance on *whether* they deliver those – not *where* they deliver them. This requires a culture of trust; we'll explore this in Chapter 5. It also requires that people are truly evaluated on their performance rather than on the time they spend in the office hunched over their screen. For all you know, that time could be spent shopping or browsing rather than doing real work! Again, evaluate the outcome not the face time.

Train your line managers to manage a flexible workforce

Another big one. Too often line managers are prejudiced against allowing co-workers actually to use their flexible time. They assume those people are skiving at home, or they feel uncomfortable that they cannot be supervising every member of their team, every minute. Here are three tips for avoiding this.

- Make sure all line managers have an open conversation with their people about how they'd like to work, and then regularly check in with them on their priorities. This makes sure both parties are aligned as to what needs to be done.
- Provide line managers with a simple Q&A guidance that gives them permission to say yes, so they don't assume they have to refuse requests in order to evidence their 'toughness', or because they feel they have to 'be in control' of their team's time or whereabouts.
- Use collaboration tools such as Google Docs, Dropbox and WorkForce so employees can share work in real time from remote locations. Use FaceTime, Skype, webinars and other tools to promote integration when working remotely.

Role-model and visibly support from the top

Make sure your senior leaders champion flexible working themselves. Be the CEO who admits she is popping off from the conference call for bathtime. Be the CFO who leaves meetings to pick up children, attends school plays or refuses to have conference calls at 6 p.m. family time. You'd be amazed what senior role-modelling can do to destigmatize flexible working. WPP's CEO Mark Read admits that he sometimes struggles to get his head around these behaviours, but knows they're the way to attract the right talent.

At CMI we all work flexibly. It starts with me, the CEO. I regularly let the team know that I'm working from home, perhaps with my dog Mudge next to me. I'm happy to share that I have fruitful phone conversations while walking to Hammersmith Bridge. At all our staff briefings I encourage others to follow my lead.

Sometimes people need encouragement. We have a talented director at CMI who came to me and confessed she was exhausted after commuting two-and-a-half hours, often rising at 4 a.m. to get to work on time. She was becoming more and more demotivated, it seemed to me, and lamented that her kids didn't recognize her any more. In a one-to-one, I probed further and it became clear that this punishing schedule was getting in the way of her work. So I asked her a simple question: who is making you do this? When she reflected, she realized that no one was; she was imposing this norm on herself. Once she knew it was absolutely fine for her to work flexibly from home, her attitude and productivity transformed!

FAQs

Here's our simple Q&A guidance for line managers about encouraging flexible working. It's been very useful in overcoming resistance at CMI and boosting support from line managers.

Q *My team member has asked to come in late on Thursday as they need to book a doctor's appointment. What do I do?*

A Say yes, unless the timing clashes with an important meeting, in which case, ask if the appointment can be rescheduled. If it can't, say yes.

....

Q *My team member is waiting for a fridge to be delivered, and they keep changing when they need to be at home to have it delivered – they said it would be Thursday morning and now they are saying they need Friday morning at home instead. It's really very difficult for me to plan around this. What do I do?*

A Say yes, and agree with the employee what their deliverables will be by the end of the week to make sure they can still meet them if they work from home on Friday morning.

....

Q *My team member has just said they think they can work from home more effectively than in the office on a permanent basis. What do I do?*

A This request would need to be made formally in writing to CMI as it falls within an area that would require a change to someone's employment contract. Before proposing your employee submits a formal request, suggest they talk to you or HR about what is making them think this is the situation, in case there are other ways to address it.

....

Q *One of my employees has a piece of work to complete and has asked to work from home tomorrow to complete it, as they keep getting distracted in the office. What do I do?*

A Say yes, as fewer distractions away from the office will allow them to give more focus to the task in hand.

Q *One of my team has asked to work from home on Fridays as they think they will be more effective, with fewer distractions, but last time I let them work from home, I am not sure they did any work at all. What should I do?*

A Check in with yourself – did you set clear expectations on the last day they worked from home? Can you set clear expectations of the output expected, and is there a way to see the work output as it happens on the next proposed day. If so, suggest another trial day where expectations are clearly set, and see how it goes.

Q *My team member's daughter/son/grandchild is having their sports day/Christmas play on Thursday and they would like to attend – they have asked to alter their hours of work on that day. What do I do?*

A Say yes.

Q *I know my team member who has asked to work from home tomorrow morning doesn't have an office set-up at home. What should I do?*

A Not having a dedicated office space at home does not mean that your team member can't work effectively.

Q *My team member has just asked if they can work from home each Friday, as their child's school hours have changed and they need to pick their child up from home. What should I do?*

A Say yes and agree expectations for work output on that day, or how the work will be managed across the rest of the week if they have a shorter day on Friday for a period of time.

Q *My team member's child/family member is unwell and they have asked to work from home. What do I do?*

A Say yes. It may be that the employee completes their working hours over a longer period of time, i.e. works in the morning, takes a break early afternoon and completes their workload in the evening, which enables them to balance looking after a child/family member and working from home.

Q *There is an important client meeting tomorrow, it has been planned in the diary for a number of weeks. The expert in the topic – who the client has asked to discuss it with – is my team member, who has just asked to work from home at the time of that meeting to help with some DIY around their house. What do I say?*

A Say no, as the colleague is the expert, they have been aware of the meeting for some time, and are therefore required by the business to attend the meeting instead of working from home. We trust our employees to make sure they are able to work effectively when at home, whether sitting in their dedicated office space, lounge or at their kitchen table, and that they are working in a physically safe way.

Q *One of my team has asked to work from home tomorrow but they don't have a laptop, so I need to say no, don't I?*

A We are planning to introduce having laptops available for everyone over time. In the meantime, if they have a valid reason for working from home, check in with the tech team and see if a laptop could be loaned to your team member for the day.

Q *One of my team members has asked to work from home because they don't get on with other team members that they work with. What should I say?*

A Say no, and explain that this isn't a basis for working from home in itself. Ask that they talk to you and/or HR about the situation in the office to see if there are ways to resolve it.

The great UK website Mumsnet produced their own top ten tips for encouraging flexible working, based on the practical experience of their members.[13] It echoes much of what we've already explored, but is still worth repeating.

1 Make it okay to ask.
2 Be flexible about flexibility.
3 Let men be parents too.
4 Be upfront about your commitment to flexible working.
5 Educate line and middle managers.
6 Focus on returners.
7 Have role models.
8 Be innovative about leave policies.
9 Flex for all – not just mums!
10 Measure, analyse and adjust.

Encouraging men to take parental leave can have great results. Many large companies, including Aviva and Accenture, have done this. Aviva offers men the same time off and pay for parental leave as women. They reported that in the first year, over 700 people – including almost 300 dads – took advantage of this equal parental leave policy.[14]

Last word on this to Luke Mills, an Accenture Managing Director: 'One of the biggest . . . things we've done is change our maternity leave to take advantage of shared parental leave . . . we created options for men to take four months' paid parental leave (alongside seven months for women) anytime in the child's first year. And the take-up of that has been extraordinarily high . . . Now what's happened with us is that actually having babies has just become a time-of-life thing which applies to men and women to an almost equal degree . . .'

4. An inclusive culture at every level that also engages men

> 'I think our efforts to date have been focused on helping women to navigate the system. The real progress will come when men and women change the system.'
> – Dame Cilla Snowball, Chair of the Women's Business Council

It's becoming increasingly clear that we need to change the cultures in which we work for diversity to thrive. This starts with new definitions of power and success that recognize our humanity and individuality. As Helena Morrissey says in her book *A Good Time to be a Girl*, 'We need a broader definition of power, a new feminine brand of power, rather than just fitting in awkwardly with the masculine concept.'[15]

So how do you go about creating a more inclusive culture when the (masculine) definitions of power and success have been around for centuries?

Men as change agents

> 'If you don't engage men, it's not going to happen. Men are still the majority leaders in organizations.'
> – Heather Melville, Chair, CMI Women

It's simple maths. If three-quarters of senior roles and a much higher percentage of CEO roles are held by men, we won't make progress on this issue without engaging men's support as change agents and champions. This has been a cornerstone of the 30% Club's success.

So how can we secure their commitment to the cause?

The UK Women's Business Council has a three-step process as part of its 'Men as Change Agents' toolkit. Specifically, they ask that CEOs do three visible things.

1 Personally champion the 33 per cent (in the UK) target of executive-level business leaders being women by 2020.
2 Sponsor between one and three women to achieve an executive-level role in your organization in the next three years.
3 Be an active 'change agent' and be part of the wider conversation to achieve better gender balance in UK business leadership.[16]

Championing men as agents of change

The Women's Business Council, *Financial Times* and CMI recognize men who are champions of change through programmes such as *FT* HERoes, Women's

Business Council Awards, and CMI's Men as Change Agents events.

Such awards recognize male leaders who are genuinely making a difference, including global pioneers such as Unilever's Paul Polman, Diageo's Ivan Menezes, the *Financial Times* commentator Andrew Hill and Chris Stylianou of Sky. Also in the spotlight have been FinTech leaders such as Nutmeg's Martin Stead or Workfront's Alex Shootman.

We need more national, regional and sectoral awards programmes – as well as individual company recognition programmes – that celebrate male changemakers at every level.

Men who champion gender balance broaden themselves in the process. Ian Ellington, the UK general manager of Pepsico (70 per cent women on the executive team), has commented – tongue in cheek – that he was 'learning an awful lot about shoes' by being a champion for women. He was actually making an important point: rather than indulging in pre-meeting sports banter, he is deliberately adapting his chat to subjects that women felt comfortable talking about. As one FTSE 100 female board member confided in another, 'Listen, the day my conversation with you about my new handbag is considered no less trivial than their conversation around football is the day we know we've got gender parity.'

Crucially, such behaviours must be championed by men – and women – throughout the organization, and not just at the top. As Carolyn Fairbairn of the CBI says, 'We need to highlight awareness and bring incentives, particularly to the middle layer of management who want to effect positive change but struggle to implement it.'

CMI's 'Blueprint for Balance' found that 75 per cent of men feel they should contribute to gender initiatives. As one male exec put it, 'I was hired by women . . . I would not have been hired in a conventional all-male format. It made me think that recognizing talent in diverse formats was really instructive.' Another said, 'I come from a matriarchal family and was brought up by strong female role models. As far as my girls are concerned, I want to make sure there is nothing they can't do.' He is busy rolling out Dads for Daughters Day, as championed by the United Nations' HeForShe campaign.[17]

One of the most notable programmes to encourage men to be agents of change comes, perhaps surprisingly, from the RAF. To combat discriminatory behaviours, the RAF trained more than 800 people to be 'safe havens' – people to whom others could go to report incidents where they felt harassed but were uncomfortable in reporting it to HR or their line manager for fear of retribution.

These 'Face It, Fix It' champions ensured all complaints were followed up without consequence to those who reported them. They have helped the RAF achieve a much greater understanding of acceptable behaviour.[18]

Other organizations are starting to deal more stringently with unwanted behaviour. Deloitte recently published a list of the partners who'd been kicked out for bad behaviour in a sexual or bullying context, and other large accountants quickly followed suit.[19] Accenture runs a programme called 'Inclusion begins with I'. Deloitte has the 'Ask Yourself' programme and videos to highlight unintended behaviours that exclude or offend others.[20]

It's clear that everyone must feel comfortable confronting behaviour that's wrong or inappropriate. One leading US lawyer has written a new guide on how to behave in the workplace in the Me Too era, recognizing that traditional men may struggle with the new norms. Her advice, which may seem obvious for a younger generation, is likely to resonate with senior male executives. Indeed, I know some men, uncertain about how to behave, who've asked me whether it's still okay to hug or kiss a woman colleague on the cheek. My view is always: yes, *if* both parties are expecting it and comfortable with it. If you are unsure, take your lead from your female colleague's behaviour.

If you're still in doubt, here are five new rules for the Me Too era. I don't necessarily agree with them – if you have trust, you shouldn't need these – but they might act as a good starter guide on shifting attitudes.

1 If you want to date a colleague and she says no, forget it.
2 Treat male and female colleagues equally. Shift the after-dinner drinks to breakfast and the golf games to something more inclusive.
3 Compliment wisely. You can say, 'That's a nice dress,' but you cannot say, 'You look hot in that dress.' Duh.
4 Don't subject your work colleagues to your sexual humour.
5 Don't touch. Read the body language of someone – or ask. If a woman leans in for a kiss, it's okay. If she sticks her hand out, it's not.[21]

Employees fight back

Much misbehaviour used to go unreported or unchallenged. No longer. Employees are increasingly unlikely to tolerate harassment, especially of a sexual nature, and more likely to organize collective action to call it out.

Employees are finding safety in numbers, and are coming forward with their own stories – even after they have signed non-disclosure agreements (NDAs). In fact, many governments are looking to invalidate NDAs in harassment cases – probably the right thing to do. Technology is making it easier for employees to register claims anonymously. In a recent UK case, Ted Baker's CEO was exposed after hundreds of employees used an anonymous app to register their experiences. I think cultures of inclusion will accelerate as these apps gain ground. Says Cherie Blair, 'Another thing we've seen recently is the power of collective action . . . Women are not prepared just to take it any more. [They're] calling it out instead of just accepting it, as the elders of my generation did; you just had to grin and bear it and shrug it off, you know. Challenge head on.'

The impact of changing demographics

The truth is, diversity is the future. As PwC's Heather Melville says, 'Organizations that don't get it may have high profits today but actually what they are going to lose is their talent. Their talent are making choices to go and work somewhere that is engaged and [where diversity] is embraced.'

One US-based company, Culture Amp, has modelled changing demographics in more than 100 companies in North America, Asia and Europe. It found that population shifts are happening everywhere; diverse groups are making up more of the workforce. Diversity is becoming the norm. As Culture Amp puts it, 'the future is intersectional'.

5. Sponsorship and mentoring programmes

> 'Everything we've learned at the Women's Business
> Council suggests that when you have men and women
> setting up a programme in their organizations for women
> to succeed through the ranks, from junior to senior . . .
> when men are sponsoring women to achieve and women
> are calling out their career ambitions, you can achieve
> change very quickly.'
> – Dame Cilla Snowball, Chair of the Women's Business
> Council

Successful gender balance programmes always involve an effective mentoring or sponsorship programme – usually both. But if your organization only has appetite for one, pick sponsorship.

Why? 'Mentors can build your self-esteem and provide a sounding board – but they're not your ticket to the top,' says Sylvia Ann Hewlett, author of *Forget a Mentor, Find a Sponsor*.[22] 'What you need is a sponsor – a senior-level champion who believes in your potential and is willing to advocate for that next raise or promotion.' Hewlett's widely quoted study found that sponsored women were much more able to ask for promotions and pay rises – and get them.[23]

Sponsors truly believe in the talent of their 'sponsees', hence they are much more likely to advocate for them when they are not in the room. Importantly, sponsors can also make a material difference to their sponsees because they have the political and social capital – the power – to do so.

Structured sponsorship programmes are particularly important in the Me Too era, where many senior men feel uncertain how to interact with younger women. (A recent article in *The New York Times* concluded that men of Wall Street were beginning to cut off all contact with female colleagues for fear of reprisals.)

Sponsorship is disproportionately effective for women and minority groups precisely because these groups have fewer informal opportunities for gaining access to their (mostly white, male) senior leaders.[24] As Bruce Carnegie-Brown puts it, 'Women need this sponsoring activity to give them more confidence than men generally need.'

So how does a structured sponsorship programme best work? Here is a checklist for putting one together.

1 **Start at the top and have a concrete outcome in mind.** Using the Women's Business Council definition, encourage male champions of change to sponsor between one and three women with the intention of getting them promoted to the executive committee within a finite time period (say, 18 to 24 months). This kind of goal frames the interaction – though, interestingly, most sponsor–sponsee relationships last many years.

2 **Make sponsorship an integrated part of your talent and succession programme** – and create structured interactions around business-related issues. Don't leave meetings to chance. Define the goals and outcomes from both sponsee and sponsor (say, completing a successful business initiative), especially given the importance of the sponsor believing in the sponsee's talent rather than just paying lip service. Have concrete projects with real outcomes, and give sponsors the opportunity legitimately to praise their sponsee.

3 Hold sponsors accountable for their sponsee's progress – and review this annually. Make sure the sponsor is actively advocating for their sponsee through introductions, invitations to high-level events or opportunities that the sponsee may not otherwise enjoy. It'll probably be worthwhile to have a training programme for sponsors to ensure they know what their role entails (see Vanessa's great checklist below).

4 Celebrate successes and extend the programme – down the organization to the levels below the executive committee and into middle and even junior management. Organizations with sponsorship programmes often enjoy higher engagement and a stronger talent pipeline. Given that millennials are less likely than older employees to stay in organizations, sponsorship could be a valuable source of retention.

5 Recognize there are two-way benefits – for sponsors and for your organization's culture. Sponsors gain insights from their sponsees, as well as becoming known as a 'talent magnet'. And having a visible sponsorship programme will help create a more inclusive culture, with people seeing leaders at every level advocating for those who are demonstrably different from themselves.

A checklist for sponsors

Vanessa Vallely, CEO of WeAreTheCity Network for Women, shared her checklist for sponsors at a CMI Women event in 2018.

1 Understand your sponsee's career aspirations and strengths.
2 Use your ability to navigate the organization, and your social capital, to advocate for your sponsee/s.
3 Connect your sponsee with others to enhance their visibility; network and showcase their capability.
4 Encourage your sponsee to stretch in their roles and assignments.
5 Offer advice on how to prepare for and handle certain situations; give actionable, constructive feedback.[25]

Mentoring and reverse mentoring programmes

The success factors for mentoring are similar to sponsorship. As with sponsoring, mentoring programmes are most successful when they are structured, and participants are held accountable.

Here are some guiding principles for successful mentoring.

- Mentees should have a concrete goal in mind, such as 'How can I get promoted?' or 'How can I increase my visibility within my organization?'
- Mentors and mentees should be matched according to skills and capabilities rather than randomly, and have a concrete time frame with structured interaction – say, one year – before both sides evaluate it. Structure and accountability, as well as some focus on talent development and monitoring of progress, are key.[26]
- Mentors generally operate in an advisory, coaching capacity. Their feedback will often be empathic rather than directive. They play a listening and a coaching role. Unlike sponsors, mentors expect very little in return,

although they also find the experience very rewarding and can gain many of the same benefits as sponsors in terms of insights into people who are different from themselves.

- One of the most successful cross-company mentoring programmes is run by the 30% Club. Over the past six years, it has grown to include more than 2,000 mentors and mentees, with women from 100-plus organizations. Successful programmes like these create valuable networks and connections, build confidence and help to make both mentors and mentees feel valued. CMI is working with the 30% Club to track the career impact and outcomes of this programme over time.

Reverse mentoring programmes are also very popular and successful. According to PwC's Heather Melville, they have to be done 'with somebody very senior at the top and someone who is a middle manager or even more junior. They will be open and honest. There shouldn't be any senior manager intervention in that process.

'Quite often the people at the top do not know what's really going on at the bottom because they hear what people want them to hear. [It] not only informs the senior leader but it also educates the person doing the reverse mentoring.'

Networks

Many companies sponsor women's networking groups, as do other organizations including CMI Women. These groups bring together women from within one firm or across firms for events, speakers and activities designed to foster increased development opportunities. Increasingly, these are also more structured, with talent development aspects to them and other interventions, such as sharing best practice. WeAreTheCity, Leanin.org and CMI Women all offer events and pathways to progress, and even a connection for bringing different women's networks together so they can learn best practice from each other. As I mentioned earlier, it's vital to encourage men to attend and get involved in women's networks as well.

Women's networks certainly have their place among the interventions to encourage women, build their confidence and help them progress. But in the end there is no firm evidence that they do specifically advance women. Rather, they seem to benefit individuals – valuable in itself.

Unless women's networks are formally integrated into succession and talent management programmes they'll continue to be a welcome addition to the mix rather than an effective lever for getting more female senior leaders in an organization. As Deborah Gilshan, founder of the 100% Club women's network, says, 'You can't set up a women's network in isolation to everything else. It's part of a more holistic strategy that has to be authentic.' A big growth area is for companies, networks and sector organizations to sponsor educational interventions that reach out to schools. Often they'll create mentoring relationships to encourage young girls. Among the best known in the UK are STEMettes, Code First: Girls, WISE, Women Tech Council and Code.org. There are many others in the USA.

These programmes are particularly welcome in underrepresented sectors such as STEM. It's good to see global programmes encouraging more women into STEM careers, too.

These programmes set out many practical steps, such as:

- setting targets for 50 per cent of apprentices to be female
- setting targets for female school-leavers, and

- exposing young women to opportunities early in their careers.

In Australia, there is a project under way to attract more women to teach engineering at universities. And the Girl Scouts of America have joined the effort with a much-needed roll-out of 20-plus STEM badges in subjects such as coding and robotics and race-car design.[27]

In summary

As Ivan Menezes, the CEO of Diageo and winner of the Male Champion of Change award from the UK Women's Business Council, said recently, 'The change we need to make won't happen overnight but it will happen with the right level of ambition and action.'

Ambition and action notwithstanding, all agree there is no one solution to fix this issue, as tempting as that would be. It takes sustained commitment throughout the entire organization – and beyond. Because the more organizational efforts are combined with broader efforts involving investors, governments, NGOs, campaigners, research organizations and media, the more likely they are to be amplified to the point of impact. Happily, such joined-up efforts are on the rise.

What Other Experts Say

What are some of the practices that work for organizations to help achieve gender balance?

Ivan Menezes (CEO, Diageo)

'It comes down to two things. Ambition and the commitment at the highest levels to make change happen. And the action on the ground to make that vision a reality . . . It's been essential to shape robust processes and policies to support recruitment retention and progression of talented women . . . It's been just as important to invest in the culture within the company.'

Julia Gillard (former Australian Prime Minister; Chair, Global Institute for Women's Leadership, King's College, London)

'In my experience, target setting makes a difference. You know, it's the old "what gets measured, gets done". Target setting. And then those targets being embedded in how people are evaluated as leaders.'

Paul Polman (former CEO, Unilever; Impact Champion, HeforShe)

'People will really watch you, what you say and what you do and if you're really committed. In Unilever we have our monthly reviews. We have a board that we've put in place. We created an external board, [there] was one person female when I came, now it's totally balanced with external directors. So they look at a lot of these things that the top has to set up. The second thing is that you treasure what you measure, not surprisingly. So we have rigorous score-carding and targets. I don't believe in quotas . . . but still in the company we have monthly reviews, we have rigorous follow-up. We set targets and we make that clear.'

Cherie Blair CBE, QC (Founder and Chair, Omnia Strategy; founder, Cherie Blair Foundation for Women)
'The CEO coming very proactively behind this so that it's not just seen as box ticking but really something that goes to the core values of a company . . . Men are the gatekeepers of power and they're often the source of many challenges, women say, as well as part of the solution. So it's much more about how do we get men to discuss these issues of gender and then convince them to do more? . . . They should start speaking up about this and we should see men playing a more positive, proactive role supporting women.'

Sir Philip Hampton (Chair, Hampton-Alexander Review)
'There are a lot of large companies that have really organized themselves well to develop, retain and promote those experienced/able women to senior executive roles and on to boards. It always seems to reflect one critical thing, which is leadership from the top, and the plans and organization to push that through. But we also see a lot of companies where female representation looks like tokenism.'

Carolyn Fairbairn (Director-General, CBI)
'Measurement around gender parity is important, and organizations that build metrics into performance targets and individual incentives make more progress on this important topic.'

Brenda Trenowden (Global Chair, 30% Club)
'At [the] 30% Club we believe strongly in targets and actually doing a really robust diagnostic first and understanding where

an organization's particular challenges are, because I think some companies just go out and think "all right, we're just gonna throw money at this initiative or that initiative" and they haven't really stopped and taken the time to be very thoughtful about where in their organization their challenges are. Then once you've found those areas, making executives accountable, putting some targets in place, and really trying to shift some of the biases in processes . . . I think creating some good healthy challenges when people see biases, and allowing people to call it out, but in a constructive way, really help to shift the challenges and biases. And I think, ultimately, sponsorship is absolutely critical.'

Sarah Gordon (former Business Editor, *Financial Times*)

'It's very difficult to change mindset but you can change processes. And if you change your interview process, and if you change your evaluation process and your promotion process, you can really start moving the dial . . . I think putting some money to be associated with this . . . It's just about the progress that they make, and if they don't make that progress they feel it in their bonus. And, you know, money talks in the business context as in every other context.'

Melanie Richards (Deputy Chair, KPMG UK)

'I absolutely think the beginning and end of this is data [because] people can't argue with data . . . It's understanding what goes on below the surface, so tracking how people make their way through the organization . . . having data in a macro sense on Hampton-Alexander has created some really healthy conversations for companies as to what's going on in their business versus the other companies in the sector.'

5 Five Steps You Can Take to Boost Gender Balance

| **Figure 13: 5 Steps You Can Take Today**

(1) Keep an achievement log and use it to address your own confidence gap

(2) Know how to successfully negotiate a promotion/raise

(3) Create a culture of trust – and challenge bad behaviour

5 Steps You Can Take Today

(4) Find the right network, sponsor and/or mentor

(5) Use evidence and strategies in this book to start to make a difference in your organization

> 'I think there are two things that everybody should be doing. Setting a good example in their own company: calling their own companies to account, their own teams to account, their own disciplines to account. And secondly, do something about it on a broader scale.'
> – Dame Cilla Snowball, Chair of the Women's Business Council

This final chapter explores the behaviours and techniques that *you as an individual* can practise to tackle gender imbalance. We really need this guidance. CMI's research has found that more than two-thirds of managers have had no training in diversity and inclusion, and more than half of junior managers don't feel comfortable dealing with discrimination.[1]

Though much of my advice is aimed at women, it works equally for men who are keen to get stuck in.

But it's important to remember that you are not superhuman; so don't set yourself superhuman goals. Here are the top five 'today steps'.

1 Achievement logs and confidence boosts
2 Negotiating pay and promotion
3 Creating trust cultures and calling out bad behaviour
4 Finding networks, mentors and sponsorship
5 Five steps you can take to close your company's gender pay gap

1. Achievement logs and confidence boosts

> 'I feel that I owe my own success to my belief in myself . . . and have found that confidence can be learned and developed. In fact, my own self-confidence is something I work on every day, just like going to the gym or training on the court.'
> – Venus Williams[2]

The first tip is the easiest to say and hardest to do. It's about addressing your own confidence gap. Even great women such as Michelle Obama, Christine Lagarde and Sheryl Sandberg admit to suffering from 'imposter syndrome' and doubting whether they deserved their success.

There's an important message in there. Even being aware that these amazing women suffer from similar issues should help you realize *you are not alone*. Far from it. As the fantastically talented Heather Melville says, 'We sometimes doubt our own ability and we need to get more women feeling confident within themselves – myself included.'

I've used four techniques during my career when I've felt daunted. I've also seen them work for women I mentor.

Keep an achievement log

An achievement log is a simple way of keeping a running tally on what you've accomplished. Keep this to hand when you're seeking a pay raise and/or a promotion, applying for a new job, or facing an assessment. It's an overview of everything you've accomplished in a specific period – typically, the past two years is a relevant time frame, although you might wish to tailor it to the circumstances.

Try to update your achievement log monthly. It's important to note enough detail to be convincing, to quantify wherever possible, as well as including the impact of what you've accomplished. Here are some examples of what might be in your log.

- Completed new software implementation ten days ahead of schedule and 10 per cent under budget.
- Recruited five new starters in record time, and at lower cost per hire.
- Closed five new clients at a 20 per cent increase in average revenue.
- Published lead author article in top global journal in my field of oncology.

You get the idea. It needs to be relevant and specific. You can, of course, include other softer measures, such as receiving positive feedback from direct reports or peers, but when it comes to boosting your morale an achievement log will be very helpful.

Keeping an achievement log works for a number of reasons. Firstly, it actually does make you realize what you have accomplished. And it's proven that if you write down three positive things every day you are likely to be more positive.

Secondly, you will never be 'caught off guard' in meetings when you have an opportunity to advertise your accomplishments. You will notice, I am sure, that males – alpha males especially – are very good at showcasing their achievements. Women often aren't. But if you know what your achievements are, because you are keeping a running log, then it is much easier to drop them into a relevant conversation with the people who need to know.

Lastly, an achievement log helps you to benchmark your achievement versus others. This will come in very handy when you're thinking about how best to advance your career. And your achievement log will also come in very handy when it comes to preparing your 'balance sheet', which we will review in the next section.

Don't just make it about confidence in you. Make sure that you have confidence in your organization's approach to promotion, pay and equality at work. As Deborah Gilshan says, 'Women have to work out whether they have confidence in the system rather than confidence in themselves. I don't believe women generally lack confidence in their abilities but they lack confidence in whether the system will recognize their abilities and what they are doing.'

If you think you're in a system that's stacked against you,

look at the final point in this chapter – and get your leadership team to read this book!

Fake it till you make it / pretend you're a friend

There is a way to 'trick' yourself into having a more confident, positive attitude. It's a fact that, if you put a smile on your face, you will improve your mood simply by virtue of having smiled. And it's also true that, if you tell yourself you can do it, you are much more likely to do it.

This is called 'fake it till you make it' and has been used by countless sales professionals to close deals in the face of opposition. It's also been used by Venus Williams. In her article 'Confidence Can Be Learned', the champion tennis player shares her technique. The idea here is to visualize, in your mind, concretely, your moment of triumph or success. Actually see it. This helps us to overcome our self-doubts.

Anna Jones is a very successful entrepreneur, the founder of AllBright and former CEO of Hearst UK. She shared with me how before big presentations she would practise nailing the deal in the loo mirror in her corner office. Then she'd head out to do it in real life.

Early in my career when I was told I was poor at oral presentations, I did exactly the same as Anna – I practised loads in my mirror, and then went out and did loads of presentations around Europe until I got quite good at it. The point is, if you're going to 'fake it till you make it', make sure you're really well prepared.

Another trick I use with women who underrate their achievements is to ask them once they've done their achievement log how they would respond to a friend or colleague who came to them with that list of accomplishments. Often they immediately respond, 'Oh, I'd say she was awesome!' Well, that awesome friend is YOU.

Similarly, if you're feeling like a failure or you've done something truly excruciating, ask yourself how you would advise a friend in that situation. I'm pretty sure you'd be empathetic and reassuring, telling her it's fine and that it will surely blow over. You would cut her some slack. So cut yourself some too!

Do, don't stew

When I was younger and would seize up with 'analysis paralysis' or overthinking, I would constantly repeat this mantra in my head. And then I would make a list of things I needed to do, and do them. Immediately I would feel better. I often use this advice with women who are stuck at a crossroads and feel unable to act. If you DO something, make some decisions, it's better than agonizing over inaction.

Take going for a job or a promotion. You may not get it, but if you DON'T APPLY, it's 100 per cent sure you won't get it. Whereas if you throw your hat into the ring, who knows? You might get it. Think like a man and apply for the job! As Brenda Trenowden says, 'If you're thinking about what you can do for yourself, be sure to put yourself forward much more and not be afraid of being rejected . . . [it's about] being bold and saying yes a bit more.' Remember Moya Greene's counsel too: 'There are no perfect candidates for anything.'

Apparently, there is more neuroscience to this than I realized. In their book *The Confidence Code*, Claire Shipman and Katty Kay exhort us to: 'Think less. Take Action.'[3] I can relate to that. And so, start making your list – even if it's filled with small things – and do them. I guarantee you'll feel better.

Be free to fail

Women aren't raised to learn failure as early as men. Boys are used to getting knocked down and getting up again, whereas girls aren't encouraged to engage in rough contact on the playground. I think this can easily turn girls into expecting always to be prepared and to be perfect. We are not. Just accept you will fail. Often! Learning how to fail fast and move on is an essential skill.

I have failed many times in my long and winding career, and I always share with others this fact – very candidly. I have been fired, and more than once; changed jobs, sectors, countries and husband. Each time, I have learned something positive. Indeed, I got this job, which I love, because I failed at another. At CMI we know that 95 per cent of those who work have experienced some form of crisis at work. And the other 5 per cent are lying. So go ahead. Fail. It's the only way you will learn how to bounce back.

2. Negotiating pay and promotion

Women need to learn to do this more often. You may surprise yourself with your success. I've counselled many women to use these techniques and, although they don't all work all the time, some of them DO work every time.

So here's my five-point plan on how to ask for a promotion or a raise. Try it! And if you do this regularly and get nowhere, my advice is to move on to somewhere where you'll be more appreciated.

Prepare a balance sheet

If you are applying for a promotion, use your achievement log to prepare a balance sheet that lists the requirements of the new job on the left-hand side, and your accomplishments to show that you meet those criteria on the right. It's a way of presenting your achievement log that makes it relevant for the specific job you are going for, and enables everyone to see how your skills and experiences meet the job requirements. It's an excellent tool I have used to get interviews for many jobs, including my current position.

Know why you deserve a raise or a promotion

This augments the previous point. If you're asking for a raise, do some benchmarking across your industry using available resources or your network. And always add ten to the equation. Women, especially, tend to undersell themselves.

Book a meeting to discuss it

This might be with your boss or the relevant HR person. It's fine to signal your intent or interest, but when it comes to make your pitch you want time set aside in someone's diary to be able to discuss it in a calm and prepared way. And signal your intent clearly: 'I'd like to set up a meeting to discuss what I need to do within the next six months to get a promotion and a raise.'

Know your company's gender pay gap

If it is available, be sure to use this in your ask. Look at the quartile you are in and point out the percentage of men versus women at this level, as well as the overall average pay gap in your organization. Point out that your pay rise and promotion is not only deserved, but will also help address the gender pay gap. Also know your organization's promotion and pay rise timings. Many companies only do this in 'cycles'; if you are 'out of cycle', especially in big companies, your ask is very likely to be met with a response of 'sorry, we cannot do this now'. So link your ask to your company's gender pay gap, pick your timing well, and do it in the cycle when your request can be considered. Don't expect an answer right away. Give your boss time to consult and think it over. But do agree a firm follow-up time.

Consider alternative asks

If you get a no, always ask, 'Well, then, can I agree a pathway to promotion over the next six months?' Would you like a sponsor? Greater flexibility? Work on a specific project? If you do get an immediate no, ask about the pathway – what you need to do in the next six months – but also consider what else you'd like that would improve your situation.

3. Creating trust cultures and calling out bad behaviour

There are two halves to this tip. The first is about how you behave. The second is how you hold others in your organization to account for their behaviour – especially bad behaviour.

How you behave

Be a line manager who inspires trust. CMI did some work on this and found that most people want to be trusted, respected, valued and given autonomy in their work. So aim to do that in how you manage people. Make sure you have genuine conversations with them and share your thinking – as well as asking their thinking – on a regular basis. Encourage them to be themselves, and be yourself as well. Make mistakes, admit to them, and allow them to do so as well – as long as they learn from them. Show them they are valued by taking an interest in them. Don't assume they will share your point of view automatically.

And don't micromanage them. Creating a culture of trust in those you manage will go a long way to ensuring you are inclusive. Allowing people to work flexibly – as we discussed in Chapter 4 – will also help.

Try getting you team together and discussing how people feel. Carolyn Fairbairn, the first female Director-General of the CBI, has learned lots by doing this: 'It can be powerful to convene groups of employees within an organization and ask, "How does it feel to work here?" It is one of the biggest things that an individual can do as a leader – even if they have a team of three – to get people together and understand how they are feeling. And you learn some incredibly surprising things. We have undertaken a similar exercise within the CBI recently, which has been incredibly insightful.'

How you hold others to account

Now that you've done all that, how do you call out the bad behaviour of others? This is a very tricky area, I realize, as people can be fearful of retribution. Understandably so. When I was an executive, I knew many women who felt like victims of discrimination and had excellent cases, but decided against pursuing them because they thought – rightly – that they would lose both their case and their career and be branded 'difficult'. Many non-disclosure agreements have been used to silence women and others who have been victims of harassment. Let's hope that the law will change to prevent their use in this area.

There's another movement afoot that's making it easier for employees to call out bad behaviour. It's about safety in numbers and shifting norms. There have been many recent examples of this where employees should take heart. Collective action by employees, plus growing recognition that discriminatory behaviour should not be tolerated, are on the rise. There are even apps you can use – such as STOPit and #NotMe – and petition websites such as Organise.org.uk – to report bad behaviour anonymously.

These bigger public steps make it easier for you to take smaller private ones. So if you have a boss, peer or colleague who consistently makes discriminatory remarks, then call it out. You can do so politely. You can also do so in a group. Simply gather a group of like-minded female and male colleagues – preferably those who have witnessed the incident or similar ones – and book an appointment to see the offender. When you share your feedback, focus on three things.

1 Be specific in citing the exact remark or behaviour, context and situation.
2 Focus on the specific behaviour and remark only. Don't judge (even though you might like to) the person's character or make it a personal attack on them.
3 State what the impact of the behaviour was on you and your peers in terms of how it made you feel and how it may have impacted others – if they are there alongside you or have shared their experiences with you. Avoid speculation. If possible and appropriate, use humour. It helps.

Accenture's Luke Mills advises, 'Basically just make people aware that you know . . . [Say:] "Hang on, you've slipped into a bias there, you're obviously not aware of it. But now you are aware that you *need* to be aware of it."'

If you get no positive response, go see your diversity champion if you have one (see the RAF example in Chapter 4). This might be your HR contact, or even your CEO. Remember, in today's world you have the power, technology and visibility to escalate matters.

If you're the person leading the meeting and you see this behaviour occur, then call it out! Interrupt and say, 'I think we should hear from Jane', or, 'Sarah made that point five minutes ago, I'm glad you agree with it.'

More men must start calling out inappropriate behaviour, says Cherie Blair. 'If someone says sexist things in the workplace, [they] look to the woman to complain. It's about time some of the men who come up afterwards and say, "We were embarrassed about that," say that in public. Because if a man takes a man on, they'd probably take it more seriously.'

Only by calling out these behaviours will we change them. That is particularly true of the small, unintentional things. And I guarantee that if you do this – especially as a male leader – you will be universally celebrated by your colleagues. You'll become a role model!

Calling out, challenging and changing behaviours to improve culture is everyone's business, not just the CEO's. If you shrug your shoulders, say it's just the way it is round here or it's just Ted being Ted, then you're complicit in saying it's okay. So don't. Set a new norm. It really is everyone's responsibility to lead by example on this.

4. Finding networks, mentors and sponsorship

> 'If someone asks me to sponsor or mentor them,
> I absolutely will do it if it's in my capacity, but only
> on the understanding that they're doing it for someone
> else and it's a pay-it-forward.'
> – Heather Melville, Chair of CMI Women

Networks

The good news is there are a lot of networks for women available. Many pioneers such as Vanessa Vallely and Deborah Gilshan, as well as CMI Women, have established successful cross-sectoral networks for women in the UK; in the USA, Sheryl Sandberg's 'Lean In Circles' have mushroomed into over 40,000 networks globally, involving millions of participants. And there are sector-focused networks such as Women in Journalism, which is run by my friend the formidably talented and well-connected Eleanor Mills. There are newly founded women-only clubs, such as AllBright in the UK and USA, and Wing in the USA, which focus on empowering women and strengthening their networks; even the almost hundred-year-old WACL club in London has recently redefined its purpose to promote gender equality in the marketing and communications business.

Increasingly there are networks for networks. WeAreTheCity, for example, regularly hosts events for women's networks to learn from each other, as does the Women's Network Forum. There is no shortage of opportunities for you to go out and join female-friendly networks and events that aim to help organizations and individuals to achieve better gender balance. Many women find these networks more pleasant to join than the established male-dominated networks; the snag is ensuring men are also involved.

Which ones are right for you? It depends on what you're looking for. Are you out to broaden your horizons or make primarily internal connections to increase your visibility? Are you looking for potential sponsors or a more senior mentor in your field. Or to be inspired by the good and the great? Depending on what you're after, there is most certainly a network for you. Here's a brief, by no means exhaustive, guide to women's networks.

Cross-sectoral

These tend to be open to all with a particular interest or point of view. Costs of joining are typically minimal, but they may charge a fee for attending events.

Leanin.org focuses on empowering women at all levels in organizations; CMI Women focuses on female managers and leaders; WeAreTheCity focuses on women in middle management who aspire to lead.

These networks are best for:

- spreading your wings
- gaining insight and learning from a broad base
- looking for mentors and other role models
- sharing advice on general barriers women face, and solutions
- building helpful contacts and connections externally, and
- learning new skills.

Sector-focused

Examples include: Women in Journalism; Women in Finance; Women in Tech; 100% Club; WACL in the UK; Women in Infrastructure; Financial Women's Network; Women Tech Council in the USA.

These networks are best for:

- sector-specific contacts, including finding a more senior mentor
- learning the ropes in your chosen field

- contacts that may help with job or skills in that field
- sharing common issues women face
- getting news and information on what's going on in your field, and
- getting the inside track on other companies you may wish to work for.

Conference-based

Examples include: International Women's Forum; Southbank's WOW; FORTUNE Most Powerful Women (MPW) summit; Tina Brown's Women in the World summit.

These can be very expensive. MPW costs in the thousands ($1,500 for two days, unless you're a speaker). In the USA many states do much more affordable versions, such as the Texas Conference for Women. These often attract key speakers and are cheaper, plus you may meet people you don't have to use Air Miles to stay in touch with. In the UK, *Management Today* frequently hosts Women in Business conferences regionally that are affordable and give a good breadth of speakers.

These networks are best for:

- hearing from world-famous speakers (WOW recently hosted Michelle Obama for an audience of 200; 40,000 applied), and
- gathering some of the great and the good globally.

Clubs

These offer a concrete space, as well as events and socializing. Examples include AllBright, in the UK and USA, and Wing in the USA.

AllBright also offers angel funding for entrepreneurs and the AllBright Academy, aimed at upskilling women.

Internal networks

Company-based networks are increasingly common, and often global, involving thousands of employees. They are increasingly open to men and are most effective if viewed as an essential part of talent management. Examples include: Breakthrough Women's Network at Lloyds Banking Group; Women in Microsoft; Women in Aviva; Women in Deloitte.

These networks are best for:

- making internal connections
- seeking out internal role models and potential sponsors, and
- building common ground and momentum for approaching gender balance at your place of work.

Mentoring

Most of us have had one or more mentors in our careers. We turn to these people for trusted advice. Mentors are a great source of objective wisdom and challenging questions. But done more formally, and with a specific 'task' or objective in mind, they can be even more useful in helping you to advance. Several women I've mentored have aspired to be promoted within a specific, six-month time frame. And most of them have succeeded. Research says women benefit from and appreciate formal mentoring more than men.

So how do you find the right mentor for you? And how do you be a good mentee?

If your company has a formal, internal, structured mentoring scheme, or a cross-company one such as the 30% Club, join it! You are one of the lucky ones. You will be matched on the basis of what your ask or objective is, rather than simply your personality. If your company doesn't have a scheme, why not investigate the kinds of women's networks mentioned above?

Sponsorship

Before you start exploring sponsorship, remember, you have to earn sponsorship through the quality and calibre of your work. You also have to be ready and comfortable with being visible. Only then can you pose the important questions: how do you find a sponsor? And how do you be a good sponsee?

Here are some DOs and DON'Ts, adapted from Vanessa Vallely's inspirational session at a 2018 CMI Women event.

- DO look for someone who knows you well enough to be able to genuinely advocate for you.
- DO look for influencers and navigators with the social and political capacity to 'make it happen' in your organization.
- DO look for someone bold enough to help remove barriers / clear a path for you.
- DON'T look for a lip-service person.
- DON'T choose someone who is sponsoring you for the wrong reasons.
- DON'T choose someone who doesn't know what good sponsorship is (see Chapter 4 for more information on this).

You yourself must be ready for sponsorship. Are you ready to be challenged? To take a new stretch assignment? Do you have your story ready and know where you want to go? Do you have your CV ready?

Heather Melville recalls how when her sponsor, Andy

Woodfield, called her up with the ideal job, she gulped. It took her some time to really be ready for the opportunity.

Finally, ask yourself: what can you offer your sponsor? You can illuminate issues for your sponsor, whether these are professional or around the challenges you face. Your sponsor should come to understand, learn from and value the perspective of someone very different from themselves.

How to find the right sponsor

Finding the right sponsor can be crucial to career advancement. Heather Melville, Chair of CMI Women, can attest to that. At a recent CMI women's event Heather and her sponsor Andy Woodfield, a partner at PwC, took to the stage to talk about how he created the opportunity for her to land her dream job. She highlights the importance of getting involved in events that give you a chance to widen your network.

Heather and Andy both agree that it was their shared interest in diversity that led to their partnership; they had judged awards together, and sat on panels together in the past. 'It's really all about doing the things outside of work that give you the exposure,' says Heather.

For Andy, it was Heather's passion and involvement and, more than anything, her values that made him realize he wanted to work with her – in fact, he designed a role specifically to suit her skillset, which he got to know in a series of conversations. He redefined the role to play to Heather's strengths. Andy put her forward and then went off on sabbatical. But of course he had sowed all the right seeds before he left, and he kept sending her encouraging texts while she was going through the process. Heather points out that great sponsors will do that for you.

If your company has a structured sponsorship programme,

apply to join it! And if your company doesn't? Consider lobbying to start one. Or, if you have the authority, simply start one. I recently spoke at a partners' breakfast for Deloitte where they realized they needed to do just that.

Don't forget to pay it forward. In the end, changing culture to be more inclusive is also about people being more willing to help each other. As Cilla Snowball reminds us, 'You're never too young to be a role model or too old to need one. We all need people to look up to. Men and women.'

5. Five steps you can take to close your company's gender pay gap

My final piece of advice centres on how you can use this book to help make a difference in your organization. My hope is that you can and will do just that, using some of the practical tips and tools included here.

So here is step-by-step advice on what to do next.

1 **Pull together a presentation** – using the infographic summaries and various 'expert quotes' included in each chapter to lend gravitas and credibility. And please DO refer to all the endnotes and resources, to download and make use of the various studies included. Start by making sure that you and your organization understand the business case for gender balance. This is outlined in Chapter 1.

2 **Benchmark your company's gender pay gap** – using the metrics set out in Chapter 2. If you're in the UK and your company has more than 250 employees you can

go on to the website gender-pay-gap.service.gov.uk and look up all the information. If you're not in the UK, ask your HR department to provide the information required of companies in the UK, once they've understood the business case and the lack of progress shared in Chapters 1 and 2. Make sure you understand your organization's own particular 'glass pyramid' issues.

3 **Discuss the pitfalls** – we shared these in Chapter 3. Are there issues that are particularly prevalent in your organization? If so, what are they? You might consider doing a survey, or conducting several focus groups in your team, division or company. Think too about which of the business case issues is most likely to resonate with your organization.

4 **Pull together a plan** – using the tips and techniques suggested in Chapter 4. Share this with your CEO, executive committee and board. If you don't have access, join together with like-minded individuals and ask politely and constructively for the chance to share it. Make sure you get as much buy-in at every level for what you are doing. And get your company to commit to targets and to measuring the programme's success over a finite period. Use the case study examples provided for guidance; and research more! Make sure you also practise the individual advice in this chapter, and share it with others.

5 **After a year evaluate your progress** – have you moved the needle? I hope so! Have you not? Why not? Share your findings, and repeat steps 1 to 5 until you do. If

after a couple of years you have made no progress, it's
time to join an organization where you can!

In summary

Gender balance has only recently taken centre stage. It certainly
wasn't discussed when I first started my career as a young MBA
more than thirty years ago. Back then, at business school, finance and investment banking were the watchwords of the day;
master them and you were a shoo-in for the top of the tree.
My hope is that these are replaced – now and for the next fifty
years – by gender balance, and the resulting inclusive culture, as
the number one drivers when defining and building a sustainable business and a successful career. The individuals, teams or
organizations that achieve true gender balance will see impacts
far greater than the accumulation of wealth on a balance sheet.
You'll be a richer person for it. You'll make better decisions, be
a better leader and get better results. You'll enjoy your work
more every day and sleep better at night. You'll make the world
a place of greater opportunity for the next generation. What a
legacy!

My aim with this book has been to give you a simple blueprint for how best to build your own legacy in this space. I hope
you've benefited from it and are inspired to combine ambition
with action. The rest is up to you.

Good luck! I'd love to hear how you get on. Do get in touch
at: ceo@managers.org.uk.

What Other Experts Say

What can individual women and men do to help achieve progress in gender balance for themselves and their organizations?

Dame Cilla Snowball (former group Chairman and group CEO, AMV BBDO; Chair, Women's Business Council, UK)

'Well I think this is an issue that everybody cares about. So, I think there are two things that everybody should be doing. Setting a good example in their own company. Calling their own companies to account, their own teams to account, their own disciplines to account. And secondly, do something about it on a broader scale.'

Paul Polman (former CEO, Unilever; Impact Champion, HeforShe)

'I would say for the first thing, as far as women are concerned, be authentic, be yourself . . . Too many women feel forced to be someone else in order to advance their careers. I'd say first of all be authentic, be yourself. Don't change. We need your style . . . Help other women is probably my second advice via mentoring or networks, holding the door open – support and encourage – you know, that type of thing. On the men's side it's a little bit more difficult because I think there's a lot of things that need to happen there. I have a lot of sympathy for men . . . [They] need to physically stand up and so, by standing up, you commit, and then by committing you hold yourself to a higher standard of behaviour. So signing up for HeforShe, [men need to] think that these are important things. Men need to also understand and be able to explain that it's not a zero-sum game – that we all win when women are supported. It's as good for men as it is for women.'

Moya Greene, (former CEO, Royal Mail, UK and Canada)

'I think to get women through these processes, it falls to people like me at this stage and age in my career – I'm sixty-four years old now – I've been a CEO for fourteen years on both sides of the pond. So it falls to women like me to say to these women, "Go through that process." Even if you don't get it the first time.'

Heather Melville OBE (Chair, CMI Women; Director of Client Experience, PwC)

'We all have a responsibility to share best practice with each other, whether it be mentorship, but mentorship cannot be on its own. We will need to sponsor people . . . it's really important that we also go and share some of our learnings in the schools and the colleges and universities. So I think the whole piece is really communication. How we do that communication and who we communicate with are really the big drivers behind all of this. And the whole piece of giving back.'

Melanie Richards (Deputy Chair, KPMG UK)

'I think just spending a little bit more time understanding the perspective of the other – and this isn't just exclusive to gender, it is all about how we make our organization more inclusive. And making assumptions that we won't be able to help those people, or see it. Or making sure that we see things from their perspective.'

Julia Gillard (former Australian Prime Minister; Chair, Global Institute for Women's Leadership, King's College, London)

'I think we are in a change moment and that community sentiment is shifting. As that happens and there is a new energy, a new wave, our task really is to harness that and make sure that we've got the practical solutions so that the change energy can then pound on and make sure it happens.'

Sarah Gordon (former Business Editor, *Financial Times*)

'I honestly don't think there's anything that women should be doing at this point. It's all about what's happening in schools and it's [about] what men can do. And, you know, not enough men are doing enough. You know, it's all very well to say women should aspire and women should do that and we have this problem with women at the top's confidence . . . Well, I don't think they need to change. I think it's the organizations, which are generally still run by men, which need to change. And it's the education that we give our children that needs to change.'

Bruce Carnegie-Brown (President, CMI; Chairman, Lloyd's of London)

'I think, put yourself in the way of opportunity. That's what you've got to do . . . and opportunity comes to people who do well in what they're currently doing. I think there's a virtuous circle around that, but as soon as you hesitate and ask yourself that question, am I ready? I think you put yourself further down the list, the queue . . . so I think you have to put yourself in the way of opportunity and give up on your doubts about yourself.'

Endnotes

Introduction: Why this book?

1 McKinsey Global Institute, 'The Power of Parity: How advancing women's equality can add $12 trillion to global growth', September 2015, p. 1.

2 PwC Global, 'Winning the Fight for Female Talent', March 2017.

3 FRC report, 'Board Diversity Reporting', September 2018, p. 9.

4 Jenny M. Hoobler et al., 'The Business Case for Women Leaders', *Journal of Management*, Vol. 44, No. 6, 2473–99, p. 2473.

5 WEF, The Global Gender Gap Report 2018, December 2018, pp. vii and viii.

6 Egon Zehnder, 2018 Global Board Diversity Tracker, December 2018, p. 14.

Chapter 1: The Business Case for Gender Equality at Work

1 Receiving the UK Women's Business Council Male Change Agent Award, Guildhall, London, 22 November 2018.

2 WEF, The Global Gender Gap Report 2017, November 2017, p. viii.

3 WEF, The Global Gender Gap Report 2018 December 2018, pp. 9 and 15.

4 Mckinsey Global Institute, 'The Power of Parity', September 2015, Executive Summary, p. 2.

5 McKinsey & Company, 'Delivering through Diversity', January 2018, p. 3.

6 Peter Dizikes, 'Study: Workplace Diversity Can Help the Bottom Line', *MIT News*, 7 October 2014, citing Sara Ellison's 'Diversity, Social Goods Provision, and Performance in the Firm'.

7   Women Financial Advisors Forum, 'Gender Diversity is a Competitive Advantage', 12 May 2016.

8   Credit Suisse Research Institute, 'The CS Gender 3000: The Reward for Change', September 2016, p. 4.

9   MSCI, 'The Tipping Point: Women on Boards and Financial Performance', 13 December 2016.

10 Paul Polman commenting on the 2017 WEF report, Unilever.com website.

11 Bloomberg, 2019 Gender-Equality Index (GEI), January 2019.

12 Government Equalities Office and Deloitte, 'Trailblazing Transparency', 2016, p. 28.

13 Opportunity Now, 'Inclusive Leadership from Pioneer to Mainstream', BITC, 2016, Executive Summary, p. 4.

14 CMI with Top Banana, Quality of Life Survey, 'Middle Manager Lifeline' report, September 2016.

15 Joep Hofhuis et al., 'Diversity climate enhances work outcomes through trust and openness in workgroup communication', SpringerPlus, 2016, Vol. 5, No. 1, p. 714.

16 GEO and Deloitte, 'Trailblazing Transparency', p. 32.

17 Michelle McSweeney, '10 Companies Around the World That Are Embracing Diversity in a BIG Way', Social Talent, 7 August 2016.

18 Cloverpop, 'Hacking Diversity with Inclusive Decision-Making', 2018, p. 6.

19 Sylvia Ann Hewlett, Melinda Marshall and Laura Sherbin, 'How Diversity Can Drive Innovation', Harvard Business Review, December 2013.

20 David Rock and Heidi Grant, 'Why Diverse Teams Are Smarter', Harvard Business Review, 4 November 2016.

21 Rock and Grant, 'Why Diverse Teams Are Smarter'; and similar findings in Katherine W. Phillips, 'How Diversity Makes Us Smarter', Scientific American, 1 October 2014.

22 Cass Business School on behalf of AIRMIC, 'Road to Ruin', 2011, p. 6.

23 CMI, 'Managers and their Moral DNA: Better Values, Better Business', 2014.

24 Lindsay Fortado, 'Hedge Funds Run by Women Outperform', *Financial Times*, 11 March 2017.

25 PwC Global, 'Winning the Fight for Female Talent', March 2017, p. 3.

26 PwC Global, 'Winning the Fight', p. 4

27 PwC Global, 'Winning the Fight', p. 7.

28 PwC Global, 'Winning the Fight,' p. x; Robert Walters, 'Future Talent Strategies, Gender Diversity and Leadership', 2018, p. 5.

29 CMI, 'The Power of Role Models', 1 May 2014; as well as PwC Global, 'Winning the Fight', p. x.

30 Catalyst, 'Quick Take: Why Diversity and Inclusion Matter', 1 August 2018.

31 Noshua Watson and Great Place to Work, 'These Tech Companies Are Leading the Change Needed for Closing the Gender Gap', *Fortune*, 30 October 2018.

32 Bloomberg, 2019 Gender-Equality Index, January 2019.

33 'The Walt Disney Company Recognised for Diversity Leadership', Disney website post, 16 December 2014.

34 TELUS International, 'How customer service significantly improves with diversity in the workplace', *Outsourcing-Today*, 7 December 2017.

35 Cressida Dick interview, *Evening Standard*, 2 November 2018.

36 'Bloomberg Gender-Equality Index Doubles in Size, Recognizing 230 Companies Committed to Advancing Women in the Workplace', Bloomberg, 16 January 2019.

Chapter 2: Five Snapshots of Global Gender Progress

1 'Time's Up: Michelle Williams praises Mark Wahlberg donating reshoot fees', *Guardian*, 14 January 2018.

2 CMI analysis of pay in annual reports 2017/18, done 4 September 2018.

3 CMI/XpertHR Salary Survey Data, 2013-17.

4 Sarah Gordon, 'Gender pay gap reporting one year on', *Financial Times*, 28 December 2018.

5 Tom Schuller, *The Paula Principle: How and Why Women Work Below Their Level of Competence*, Scribe, 2017.

6 Catalyst, 'Women in S&P 500 Companies', 2018.

7 PwC Global, 'Winning the Fight for Female Talent', March 2017, p. 5.

8 McKinsey & Company, in partnership with LeanIn.Org, 'Women in the Workplace 2018', October 2018, p. 5.

9 Grant Thornton, 'Women in business: beyond policy to progress', March 2018, p. 4.

10 Grant Thornton, 'Women in business', p. 8.

11 Hampton-Alexander Review, November 2018, p. 4.

12 Catalyst, 'Leadership Quick Take', 21 October 2018.

13 Egon Zehnder, 'Who's really on board', December 2018, p. 14; Hampton-Alexander Review, p. 13.

14 Sarah Gordon, Aleksandra Wisniewska and Billy Ehrenberg-Shannon, 'UK gender pay gap reporting one year on', *Financial Times*, 28 December 2018. (Based on just under 700 out of 10,000-plus companies required to report.)

15 Andrew MacAskill and William James, 'HSBC has worst gender pay gap among Britain's largest companies', Reuters, 4 April 2018.

16 Cranfield School of Management, 'Moving on up: a gender perspective for practical inclusive talent management for senior roles', 2018.

17 McKinsey & Company, 'Closing the gap: Leadership perspectives on promoting women in financial services', September 2018.

18 Catalyst, 'Quick Take: Women in Science, Technology, Engineering, and Mathematics (STEM)', 3 January 2018.

19 Meaghan Ouimet, '5 Numbers that Explain Why Stem Diversity Matters to All of Us', *Wired*, 5 May 2015.

20 Blanca Myers, 'Women and Minorities in Tech by the Numbers', *Wired*, 27 March 2018.

21 McKinsey & Company, 'The Power of Parity: Advancing women's equality in the United Kingdom', September 2016, pp. 27 and 53–4.

22 Josh Jacobs, 'Macho brogrammer culture still nudging women out of tech', *Financial Times*, 10 December 2018.

23 Sam Levin, 'Google gender pay gap: women advance suit that could affect 8,300 workers', *Guardian*, 26 October 2018.

24 Anna Johansson, 'Why Millennials are Demanding Even More Diversity in Tech', *Forbes*, 19 December 2017.

25 MSCI, Women on Boards Progress Report, December 2018, pp. 3–4.
26 Susan E. Reed, 'Corporate boards are diversifying. The C-suite isn't', *Washington Post*, 4 January 2019.
27 World Economic Forum, The Global Gender Gap Report 2018, p. vii.
28 World Economic Forum, The Global Gender Gap Report 2017, p. 28.
29 Dame Laura Cox DBE, 'The Bullying and harassment of Commons Staff: Independent Inquiry Report', 15 October 2018, p. 69.
30 Adam Sage, 'How misogyny, infidelity and betrayal destroyed Ségolène Royal's bid to become president of France', *The Times*, 10 November 2018.
31 Pew Research Center, '10 things we learned about gender issues in the U.S. in 2017', 28 December 2017.
32 'Bloomberg Gender-Equality Index Doubles in Size, Recognizing 230 Companies Committed to Advancing Women in the Workplace', Bloomberg, 16 January 2019.
33 Emma Wills, 'Iceland has made it illegal to pay women less than men', *Evening Standard*, 3 January 2018.
34 Grant Thornton, 'Women in business', p. 8.
35 Equileap, Gender Equality Global Report and Ranking, 2018 Edition, p. 7.
36 'Bloomberg Gender-Equality Index Doubles in Size', January 2019.
37 Hampton-Alexander Review, November 2018, p. 2.

Chapter 3: The Top Five Pitfalls Preventing Gender Balance

1 Caoilfhionn Raleigh, 'The Effects of the Perceived Glass Ceiling on Women's Psychological Well-Being from an Experienced Incivility Perspective', unpublished thesis, August 2018.
2 Tom Knowles, 'Google sacks 48 staff for sexual harassment', *The Times*, 26 October 2018.
3 Kaya Burgess, 'Groping and sexism "fuelled by free alcohol at WeWork office parties"', *The Times*, 20 October 2018.
4 Melissa Davey, 'Australian report finds disturbing evidence of gender inequality', *Guardian*, March 2017.

5 FRC, 'Board Diversity Reporting', September 2018, p. 2.

6 Frank Dobbin and Alexandra Kalev, 'Why Diversity Programmes Fail', *Harvard Business Review*, July–August 2016.

7 Matthew Moore, 'Pale, stale Mad Men at JWT claim discrimination', *The Times*, 13 November 2018.

8 For examples see Christine Armstrong's book, *The Mother of All Jobs* (Bloomsbury, 2018).

9 CMI Women, 'A Blueprint for Balance: Time to fix the broken windows', January 2018, p. 24.

10 CMI Women, 'A Blueprint for Balance', p. 24.

11 Institute for Fiscal Studies, 'Mothers suffer big long-term pay penalty from part-time working', 5 February 2018.

12 Zlata Rodianova, 'Working mums: over half of British mothers think their children prevent them from getting a better job', *Independent*, 25 February 2016 (quoting Mumsnet survey, 2015).

13 Kate Elliot, 'The Fatherhood Bonus and the Motherhood Penalty', *Augsburg Now*, 16 November 2017, featuring the work of academic Michelle Budig of the University of Massachusetts.

14 CMI Women, 'A Blueprint for Balance', p. 21; plus the work of Dr Heejung Chung, University of Kent.

15 CMI Women, 'A Blueprint for Balance', p. 21.

16 CMI Women, 'A Blueprint for Balance', p. 20.

17 From Christine Armstrong's speech at *Management Today*'s Inspiring Women's Conference, London, 1 November 2018.

18 Steve Warnham, Total jobs recruiter blog, 13 November, 2017; Danielle Gaucher et al., 'Evidence that Gendered Wording in Job Advertisements Exists and Sustains Gender Inequality', *Journal of Personality and Social Psychology*, 2011, Vol. 101, No. 1, 109–28.

19 Iris Bohnet, 'The Promise of Behavioral Design', in *What Works* (Harvard University Press, 2016).

20 Paola Cecchi-Dimeglio, 'How Gender Bias Corrupts Performance Reviews, and What to Do About It', *Harvard Business Review*, 12 April 2017.

21 Aine Cain, '5 years after Facebook exec Sheryl Sandberg's famous book told women to "lean in," it appears that advice may have mixed results', *Business Insider*, 6 August 2018.

22 Dobbin and Kalev, 'Why Diversity Programmes Fail'.

23 Lisa Rabasca Roepe, 'Are Female-only Networks Hurting Women in the Workforce?' OZY, *The Daily Dose*, 15 May 2017.

24 Will Kirby, 'Out of touch! Fury as pay gap review chief claims BBC women "let it happen"', *Daily Express*, 27 July 2017.

25 Helena Morrissey, *A Good Time to be a Girl* (Bloomsbury, 2018), p. 42.

26 Kate Clark, 'Female founders have brought in just 2.2% of US VC funding this year (yes, again)', TechCrunch, November 2018.

27 Emma Jacobs interview, 'Sarah Cooper: The workplace is a rich seam for comedy', *Financial Times*, 24 October 2018.

Chapter 4: Five Practices That Work for Organizations

1 Hampton-Alexander Review, 'FTSE Women Leaders: Improving gender balance in FTSE leadership', November 2018, p. 37.

2 Quoted in Bloomberg's 2019 Gender-Equality Index, 16 January 2019.

3 Women's Business Council, 'Five Years On Progress Report 2018', p. 33.

4 Henry Sanderson, 'BHP on track to achieve 50% female workforce by 2025', *Financial Times*, 16 October 2018.

5 'Lululemon achieves equal pay for women', Makers, 10 April 2018.

6 David Silverberg, 'Why do some job adverts put women off applying?', BBC News website, 12 June 2018.

7 Government Equalities Office, 'Reducing the gender pay gap and improving gender equality in organisations: Evidenced-based actions for employers', 2018.

8 The GEO report, CMI Women's 'A Blueprint for Balance', Women's Business Council's 'The Pipeline Effect' toolkit and the PwC report 'Winning the Fight for Female Talent' are all in the resources section and available free online.

9 Global Institute for Women's Leadership, King's College London, Report on Progression, November 2018.

10 PwC Global, 'Winning the Fight for Female Talent', March 2017, p. 23.

11 Adapted from Women's Business Council, 'Returners: A Toolkit for Employers', March 2018, pp. 5–7.

12 CIPD, 'Flexible Working: the business case', November 2018.

13 Mumsnet Jobs, 'Ten recommendations to make flexible working work for employers', Mumsnet, 2018.

14 Caroline Prendergast, 'Equal paid parental leave benefits all workers, Aviva shows', *Financial Times*, 20 November 2018.

15 Morrissey, Helena, *A Good Time to be a Girl* (Bloomsbury, 2018), p. 83.

16 Women's Business Council, 'Men as Change Agents' toolkit, 2018.

17 CMI Women, 'A Blueprint for Balance: Time to fix the broken windows', January 2018, p. 29.

18 CMI Women, 'A Blueprint for Balance', p. 27.

19 Madison Marriage, 'Big Four auditors reveal number of partners fired over misbehaviour', *Financial Times*, 11 December 2018.

20 See the videos on YouTube. They include a number of remarks and also how they impact people.

21 Joan Williams, 'Five rules for the office in the #MeToo era', *Financial Times*, 19 October 2018.

22 sylviaannhewlett.com/.find-a-sponsor-html.

23 Sylvia Ann Hewlett, 'The Real Benefit of Finding a Sponsor', *Harvard Business Review*, 26 January 2011.

24 Center for Women and Business at Bentley University, 'Mentorship, Sponsorship, and Networks: The Power and Value of Professional Connections', September 2017, p 4. (The Bentley study found men's networks and senior exec interaction was more frequent than women's.)

25 Adapted from a talk, 'What Sponsorship Is, and Isn't', by Vanessa Vallely OBE at CMI Women, 21 November 2018.

26 Catalyst, 'Report: Making Mentoring Work', 19 January 2010, p. 1.

27 '23 new STEM and outdoor badges', www.girlscouts.org, 25 July 2017.

Chapter 5: Five Steps You Can Take to Boost Gender Balance

1   CMI, managers' voice survey, conducted January 2019.

2   Venus Williams, 'Confidence Can Be Learned', *The New York Times*, 6 December 2018.

3   Claire Shipman and Katty Kay, *The Confidence Code: The Science and Art of Self-assurance – What Women Should Know* (HarperBusiness, 2014).

Further reading and resources

Please also check the endnotes.

Research reports

Bloomberg, 2019 Gender-Equality Index (GEI), January 2019.

Catalyst, 'Quick Take: Why Diversity and Inclusion Matter', 1 August 2018.

Catalyst, 'Quick Take: Women in Management', 30 July 2018.

Catalyst, 'Quick Take: Women in Science, Technology, Engineering, and Mathematics (STEM)', 3 January 2018.

Catalyst, 'Quick Take: Women on Corporate Boards', 21 December 2018.

Center for Women and Business at Bentley University, 'Mentorship, Sponsorship, and Networks: The Power and Value of Professional Connections', September 2017.

CIPD, 'Flexible Working: the business case', November 2018.

CMI with the British Academy of Management, 'Delivering Diversity: Race and ethnicity in the management pipeline', July 2017.

CMI Women, 'A Blueprint for Balance: Time to fix the broken windows', January 2018.

Committee for Perth, 'Filling the Pool' report and roadmap, June 2015.

Cranfield School of Management, 'Moving on up: a gender perspective for practical inclusive talent management for senior roles', 2018.

Cranfield School of Management, 'The Female FTSE Board Report', 15 July 2018.

Credit Suisse Research Institute, 'The CS Gender 3000: The Reward for Change', September 2016.

Culture Amp, 'Diversity, Inclusion, and Intersectionality Report: Insights into the world of diversity and inclusion', 2018.

Frank Dobbin and Alexandra Kalev, 'Why Diversity Programmes Fail', *Harvard Business Review*, July–August 2016.

Egon Zehnder, 2018 Global Board Diversity Tracker, December 2018.

Equileap, Gender Equality Global Report and Ranking, 2018 Edition.

FRC, 'Board Diversity Reporting', September 2018.

Global Institute for Women's Leadership, King's College London, Report on Progression, November 2018.

Government Equalities Office: Actions to Close the Gender Pay Gap, 'Reducing the gender pay gap and improving gender equality in organisations: Evidence-based actions for employers', 2018.

Grant Thornton, 'Women in business: beyond policy to progress', March 2018.

Hampton-Alexander Review, 'FTSE Women Leaders: Improving gender balance in FTSE leadership', November 2018.

Jenny M. Hoobler et al., 'The Business Case for Women Leaders: Meta-Analysis, Research Critique, and Path Forward', *Journal of Management*, Vol. 44, No. 6, 2473–99.

Institute for Fiscal Studies, 'Mothers suffer big long-term pay penalty from part-time working', 5 February 2018.

McKinsey & Company, 'Closing the gap: Leadership perspectives on promoting women in financial services', September 2018.

McKinsey & Company, 'Delivering through Diversity', January 2018.

McKinsey & Company, 'The Power of Parity: Advancing women's equality in the United Kingdom', September 2016.

McKinsey & Company, 'Women in the Workplace 2018', October 2018.

McKinsey Global Institute, 'How advancing women's equality can add $12 trillion to global growth', September 2015.

MSCI, 'The Tipping Point: Women on Boards and Financial Performance', 13 December 2016.

MSCI, Women on Boards Progress Report 2018, December 2018.

Pew Research Center, '10 things we learned about gender issues in the U.S. in 2017', 28 December 2017.

PwC Global, 'Winning the Fight for Female Talent: How to gain the diversity edge through inclusive recruitment', March 2017.

Robert Walters, Empowering Women in the Workplace, 'Future Talent Strategies: Gender, Diversity and Leadership', 2018.

David Rock and Heidi Grant, 'Why Diverse Teams Are Smarter', *Harvard Business Review*, 4 November 2016.

Timewise in partnership with EY, 'Flexible Working: A Talent Imperative', 19 September 2017.

Women's Business Council, 'Five Years On Progress Report 2018: Maximising women's contribution to future economic growth', 2018.

World Economic Forum, The Global Gender Gap Report 2018, December 2018.

Case studies and toolkits

Accenture, 'When She Rises, We All Rise. Getting to Equal 2018: Creating a culture where everyone thrives', 2018.

Business in the Community, Diversity Benchmark service, 2019.

CMI Diversity and Inclusion Accreditation Standard.

Mumsnet Jobs, 'Ten recommendations to make flexible working work for employers', Mumsnet, 2018.

Silicon Republic, '5 Case Studies of Companies Trying to Correct the Gender Pay Gap', 28 November 2018.

Kea Tijdens, 'Promoting Gender Equality in the Workplace: Case Studies from the Netherlands', University of Amsterdam, August 2000.

WISE Campaign (Women into Science and Engineering), www.wisecampaign.org.uk/.

Women's Business Council, 'Balance the System: How to increase gender diversity to accelerate business growth', 2018.

Women's Business Council, 'Men as Change Agents', 2018.

Women's Business Council, 'Returners: A Toolkit for Employers', 2018.

Women's Business Council, 'Staying On: The Age of Success' (for older women), 2018.

Women's Business Council, 'The Pipeline Effect: A toolkit for enabling gender parity beyond middle management', 2017.

Workplace Gender Equality Agency Australia, www.wgea.gov.au/.

Books

Christine Armstrong, *The Mother of All Jobs: How to Have Children and a Career and Stay Sane(ish)*, Bloomsbury, 2018.

Iris Bohnet, *What Works: Gender Equality by Design*, Harvard University Press, 2016.

Elena Favilli and Francesca Cavallo, *Good Night Stories for Rebel Girls*, Particular Books, 2017.

Sally Helgesen and Marshall Goldsmith, *How Women Rise: Break the 12 Habits Holding You Back*, Random House Business, 2018.

Sylvia Ann Hewlett, *Forget a Mentor, Find a Sponsor: The New Way to Fast-Track Your Career*, Harvard Business Review Press, 2013.

Katty Kay and Claire Shipman, *The Confidence Code: The Science and Art of Self-Assurance – What Women Should Know*, HarperBusiness, 2014.

Helena Morrissey, *A Good Time to be a Girl: Don't Lean in, Change the System*, William Collins, 2018.

Michelle Obama, *Becoming*, Viking, 2018.

Sheryl Sandberg, *Lean In: Women, Work, and the Will to Lead*, WH Allen, 2015.

Sue Unerman and Kathryn Jacob, *The Glass Wall: Success Strategies for Women at Work – and Businesses That Mean Business*, Profile Books, September 2016.

Vanessa Vallely, *Heels of Steel: Surviving and Thriving in the Corporate World*, Panoma Press, 2013.

Networks

100% Club (www.the100percentclub.co.uk)

CMI Women (www.managers.org.uk/cmi-women)

Everywoman (www.everywoman.com)

FidAR Germany (www.fidar.de)

HeforShe (www.heforshe.org)

International Women's Forum UK (www.iwforumuk.org)

Lean In (https://leanin.org)

Mumsnet (www.mumsnet.com)

My Family Care (www.myfamilycare.co.uk)

Parity.org (www.parity.org)

Speakers for Schools (www.speakers4schools.org)

UN Women (www.unwomen.org)

WACL (Women in Advertising and Communications) (https://wacl.info)

WeAreTheCity (https://wearethecity.com)

WIBN (Women in Business Network) (www.wibn.co.uk)

Women Ahead (www.women-ahead.org)

Women in Finance (www.womeninfinance.co.uk)

Women Tech Council (www.womentechcouncil.com)

Acknowledgements

Many people and organizations contributed to creating this book. I'd like to thank them here. Martina O'Sullivan, my upbeat, very-easy-to-work-with editor who approached me about this series and agreed with my pitch to do this particular book, is a good place to start. Others include my assistant Lynnette Paddy for calmly and carefully turning my misspelled prose into something more readable; Caoilfhionn Raleigh for her help with research and interview transcription; Tanya Aitkin for her slick diagrams and occasional cheerleading; and Matthew Rock for his swift and eloquent editing. A big thanks to all of my interviewees who candidly shared their thoughts, and the many individuals and organizations who champion gender balance, share their experiences and inspire me and others to help make it happen every day. Finally, thanks to my family: daughter Izzy, husband Barry and my mother, Arden – who at ninety-one remains an inspiration. And, of course, to my wonderful work family at CMI.

Acknowledgements

Index

PENGUIN PARTNERSHIPS

Penguin Partnerships is the Creative Sales and Promotions team at Penguin Random House. We have a long history of working with clients on a wide variety of briefs, specializing in brand promotions, bespoke publishing and retail exclusives, plus corporate, entertainment and media partnerships.

We can respond quickly to briefs and specialize in repurposing books and content for sales promotions, for use as incentives and retail exclusives as well as creating content for new books in collaboration with our partners as part of branded book relationships.

Equally if you'd simply like to buy a bulk quantity of one of our existing books at a special discount, we can help with that too. Our books can make excellent corporate or employee gifts.

Special editions, including personalized covers, excerpts of existing books or books with corporate logos can be created in large quantities for special needs.

We can work within your budget to deliver whatever you want, however you want it.

For more information, please contact
salesenquiries@penguinrandomhouse.co.uk